THIS is the first collecti... Christopher Morley's essa... ten years. Few writers write in this medium as affectionately, as pointedly, with such good humor, and with so much subterranean meaning as Mr. Morley. And THE IRONING BOARD is a rich, flavorful selection that will delight the Morley fans (Russel Crouse said of one of his essays: *"He has done what Burbank couldn't do, mixed sex and garden vegetables"*) and all lovers of the familiar essay.

In explaining the title, Mr. Morley puts it this way: "When a daughter was married here in the old demoted grange I bought an ironing board, covered it with a fair linen tablecloth to serve as a sideboard (in a corner of my study) for a case of Scots whiskey which I knew some of the oldtimers, congeners, kinsmen, and crapulous would prefer to the New York State Champagne. After the prothalamia were over I kept it there and decided to use it as a file for casual writing . . . So for years, I piled this and that on the ironing board, and now I am making a sombre choice. They are the things I myself like best to remember."

The Ironing Board

The IRONING BOARD

BOARD

CHRISTOPHER MORLEY

1949

DOUBLEDAY & COMPANY, INC., GARDEN CITY, N. Y.

*This book is dedicated, ultimately,
to four grandchildren:—*

    ALISON MORLEY COCHRANE

    WHITNEY WOODRUFF II

    JANET FAIRCHILD COCHRANE

    JOHN CHRISTOPHER WOODRUFF

but as residuary dedicatees.
Until they are old enough to condone
such public notification
(Say 20 years from now?)
their trustee is hereunder named
as curator of any benevolence that can accrue:—

devoted, discreet, and much enduring friend,

                LOUIS GREENFIELD

ROSLYN HEIGHTS, N.Y.
JUNE, 1949

Contents

7

The Ironing Board

The Ironing Board

SATURDAY, DECEMBER 23, 1944, WAS FOGGY AND SLEETY AND freeze-drizzling. The bridegroom (a medical midshipman) had a small furlough ration of gas, but I was worried about the roads. I took the old Blue Car down to the village pump to get salt-pads and glycerine for the windshield. Then I parked her tangent to a neighbor's drive so the young pair could make fast getaway. Yes, it was a wedding day, and the Old Man was trying to foresee everything.

He had ordered, for instance, F.O.B. (*Father of the Bride*) 5 cases, or was it 6? of N.Y. State champagne. It was certainly not as excessive an occasion as described by Mr. Ed Streeter in his riotously grievous book of that title, but it was enough, 'twould serve. And the man who did the serving, the caterer, was the only one who got cooked. In the general scarmouche (Chaucer's glorious word) after the young couple had flitted, it was the caterer who was grapeshot and did vaudeville acts.

But the Old Man knew that some of the mature bullfrogs of his clan would prefer whisky. He went to the local hardware and bought an Ironing Board. He put it in the far end of his study and draped it with a fair linen cloth. There he set out a dozen of that rare and noble Scots whisky *Loch Fyne*, with adequate ice-cubes and crystal. That was for the oldtimers. Who would have guessed that napery buvette was, underneath, just a $2.95 ironing board?

I wish there were time and space—I have the space, but have you enough time?—to recall various aftermath. The file of squirrels, early Sunday morning, trooping to the crates of broken leftovers, each carrying away to the adjoining woods his own shard or crust. But even after the wreckage of romance was cleared, remained the Ironing Board draped in flaxy linen. F.O.B. said to himself, I'll use it as a filing case. He was then working on other matters which he was silly enough to think more important, but he put on the ironing board, when he remembered, casual things he had written. They were things written, whether for anger or amusement, just because he felt that way. They got to be heavier even than the whisky, and once the board collapsed. Some things he forgot, others he never could find, but quite a pile accumulated.

It is more than ten years since he has ventured to print, or reprint, any of this plain garden salsify. He has been told, almost often enough to believe it, that he is not a novelist, nor a dramatist, nor a poet. But there is, maybe, a kind of satiric saltarello that is natural to his temper. Here are a few of them for those who relish dandelion salad.

So, on this Ironing Board, when he happened to think of it, he smoothed out scraps of copy. There were some literary

essays, some burlesque detective stories, some awkward tributes to writers he thinks of noble feeling. There were even (he
would like to think) one or two comic skits that, as the high-
minded editors said, "are not the kind of things our readers
expect from you."

An Ironing Board is where a burning metal goose passes
over the damp crumpled linen of daily life. Here, for the first
time in ten years, and what years, are some of the joys and
angers of your momentary spokesman.

Now to be specific. Professor Saintsbury, the king of literary
manners in our lifetime, always insisted it was only decent
courtesy to annotate the origins of any such collection. Many
of these pieces show obvious signs of the times or climates
in which they were written. As acknowledgement to their
first sponsors, and as information to any inquisitive reader:—

"*On Belonging to Clubs*," written in a seizure of Christmas
hilarity, was printed in *The New Colophon*, Part Six, June
1949.

Time of Life was written during that incredible spell of
heat and humidity we suffered on Long Island at the end of
July and beginning of August, 1945. The weather bureau, and
my colleagues in the local Community Garden, will confirm
my memory of that abominable spell of the vapors. I have
sometimes wondered if it might have been some reaction from
the first atom bomb explosion in New Mexico? At any rate,
two days after I mailed the script to a distinguished monthly
magazine, the bomb on Hiroshima was announced. The editor,
after a while, gently reproached me for writing what his
readers would not expect from me; he said the tale was lewd,
and that anyhow the world had now more important woes

to consider. He was quite right. I was abashed; the MS simmered and steamed on the Ironing Board for more than a year, but then '47 *Magazine* was invented and I sold it to them for half what I had subscribed for their stock. I still think it amusing, I wish it could be translated into French; I have seen just the same shimmer of earth's brute anguish over the harvest fields of Burgundy. I have of course apologized to neighbors and fellow-tillers of our old commune glebe. But I remember, in my solitary moments of self-consolation, Mr. Russel Crouse's generous remark: "You have done what even Burbank couldn't do, crossed sex with garden vegetables."

Notes on an Island, memoranda of the first visit to England in many years, was written in December 1947; printed in two chapters in the *Saturday Review of Literature*, April 17 and 24, 1948.

Saint Bypass was in '47 *Magazine*, December 1947; and also, like *Time of Life*, most gaily and stringently illustrated by Lucille Corcos, to whom my sincere homage. The great War Department Viaduct alluded to will be finished by the time this book is published. If you cross it, look down to the left, at the eastward end, and see little Saint Bypass.

The episodes of Dove Dulcet, my burlesque Secret Agent, were needled by Mr. Ellery Queen's rediscovery of that obscure comedian whom I used as filler about 1921–23 in the old New York *Evening Post*. *Codeine* was in *Ellery Queen's Mystery Magazine*, November 1945. *Hitch Your Wagon*—(still good fiscal advice) was in *EQMM* July 1947. The other two (*Murder in Red and Green*, and *The Adventure of Foggy Bottom*) have not been printed before in U.S.A., but *Foggy Bottom* was in the first issue (1949) of the *London Mystery Magazine*.

I hope a few Johnsonians will find *Another Letter to Lord Chesterfield* good parody. It was written in the great cigarette famine of 1944–45. I tried to sell it to Liggett & Myers Tobacco Company. My dear old friend Burton Emmett, who first marketed that cigarette, would have loved it, but he was dead and his successors admitted they couldn't understand a word of it. Ben Abramson, the temperamental bookseller, printed a small private edition in perfect facsimile of the eighteenth-century type of Johnson's *Lives of the Poets*. He couldn't sell it either, but his address is Mohegan Lake, N.Y.

An American Gentleman was in the *Saturday Review of Literature*, September 20, 1947, but some months earlier in the *Manchester Guardian* (England). If you send anything to the *Guardian*, and if they approve it, they print it quick.

Bronzino's Mixture, which I first called *Brentano's Mixture*, was written in autumn 1946. I tried to tell Arthur Brentano, the famous bookseller, and his associates Joe Margolies and Laurence Gomme, how valuable this might be as a brochure for their business. I offered it to them, gratis, as a Christmas gift, but they waved me away. Then I offered it, also as a professional snort, to dear old Frederic Melcher, editor of the *Publishers' Weekly*. Fred, after losing it in his desk for six months (he went to Japan to Build Up American Books), told his secretary to tell me it was too bookish.

What Happened at Quebec, a simple and honest job of reporting, must have been written in September 1944. It was printed in *Saturday Review of Literature*, September 30, 1944. It was one of the first news-stories that ventured to see F.D.R. as a dying man. I know that when he was wheeled off the terrace by his colored attendant I happened to be alongside, but

15

I forebore to speak to him. I was too troubled by his Color of Death.

Watson à la Mode I preserve because it was written for the first issue of that pursehumble quarterly *The Baker Street Journal,* January 1946. Its motto is, "When was so much written by so many for so few." *A Christmas Story without Slush* was also written for the Baker Street Irregulars.

I have included, for my own files rather than anyone else's, a few personal tributes. *The Atom Splitter,* written late in 1945, was declined by an intellectual monthly as too literary. So I put it into the 70th Anniversary Volume in honor of Dr. A. S. W. Rosenbach (Philadelphia, 1946). Then there are two birthday tributes to the two most perfect artists (in their own wave-lengths) of our lifetime, Max Beerbohm and Walter de la Mare. Then also four loveletters to old friends who have gone their ways with many years of love and laughter from me. These are E. V. Lucas (*Sat. Rev. Lit.,* July 2, 1938), Hulbert Footner (I wrote for him a preface for his last book, *Orchids to Murder;* Harper, 1945), Tom Daly (in the Philadelphia *Inquirer,* December 5, 1948), and Bob Holliday (N.Y. *Herald Tribune,* January 1947).

Let me say again, in case anyone was listening, these pieces were almost all written within the Decade of Damnation, 1939–49. Their anxieties are sometimes a little heavy, their laughter perhaps hysterical; but any analyst will see in them the struggle, not altogether unworthy, of a mind to keep itself alive. They were put down in intervals of escape from what the writer probably thought more important work. It is sad that no writer can ever enforce what his readers should like. His earliest and corniest stuff gets quoted from here to there (such as Mark Twain's Jumping Frog, which he himself loathed as a Boeotian backwoods anecdote); anything razored with the hollow Sheffield blade and the ivory handle is utterly unnoticed. The writer is the best judge; but he is not the jury.

Tempest 1941 was an attempt to find solace behind one of my two Maginot Lines, Chaucer & Shakespeare. In those horrible days of 1940 I found myself rereading *The Tempest,* and busied myself by arranging it for a possible stage. I put down the notes, here reprinted, for an introduction. Two or three years later *The Tempest* was reproduced on Broadway, but of course without much success. It is not a play for the stage, but (like Shakespeare's best) a charade for the conscience.

Galling Shakespeare's kibe comes Bacon. The introduction to the Essays was written on Leap Year Day, February 29, 1944, when I was existing weirdly in a Riverside Drive apartment and the only table writable-upon had a thick sheet of cold glass. I was always suspicious of desks so platened, and I think that my private horrors crept up from the elbow and improved the cynicism that My Lord Verulam would have relished. That is a piece I like; it draws blood; and there was blood there to be drawn. I am pleased too that in the Limited Editions Club volume (1944) my old friend Dr. A. S. W. Rosenbach made one of his few errors. He speaks of the foundering of the *Titanic* as in November 1912, but we all know (who had friends aboard) she went down—by impact with a huge nemesis of glassy ice—in April of that year. It is so comforting to find Dr. Rosy and the Limited Editions Club in an error that I venture to mention it. That is, as the American News Company shrewdly says, not a book, nor an "essay," for everyone.

The Sense of Place was written, by request, for a volume called *Literary England;* an albumen of excellent photos taken for *Life* magazine by David E. Scherman and Richard Wilcox.

It was a "picture essay" in *Life*, June 14, 1943, and subsequently published as book by Random House with my preface added. Hazlitt would have liked it, but no one else ever did, so I think I have a right to recapture it for my own musette bag.

Weeding Beets, another memory of those terrible days in the Community Garden, was printed in the 20th anniversary issue of the *Saturday Review of Literature*, August 5, 1944.

The Consolable Widow was one of my from-time-to-time series of adaptations from Bataille's *Causes Criminelles et Mondaines* (the greatest treasury in print of criminal trials) and was printed by Ellery Queen in his *Mystery Magazine*, May 1946. I have long wanted to do some more drainages from Bataille (the only Bataille that Larousse mentions is *Henry*, 1872–1922, "psychologue subtil et hardi, parfois morbide"; but that would apply to Albert Bataille also). My Bataille is *Albert*. He doesn't make comedy (as did Roughead and his disciple Edmund Pearson) of human horrors; he lifts it into the higher realm of the spiritual-sardonic. There isn't anything very funny about murdering or being murdered.

I have included, with some hesitation, a letter written with no intention of print. The Christmas message to that great and kind man T. W. Lamont was written to give him a glimpse of what was going on at Canterbury Cathedral, to which (for repairs) he had given an enormous generosity. He wrote me, only a few days before his death, that he hoped I would print the letter somewhere, some time. I regard that as a mandate.

On Belonging
to Clubs[1]

I WOKE UP JUST NOW LAUGHING AND TALKING TO MYSELF. It must have been amusing, because I heard acoustic (and caustic) whispers from upstairs. "Quiet! You'll wake the baby." (A grandson, here on visit.)

I am a collector of risibilia, and I have two recurring dreams that always take me comic. They come mostly in what Oscar Firkins called "the warm little hollow between Christmas and New Year."[2] Then, by overeating and overreading, the triple expansion impulse-reaction turbines of the mind[3] slip a few steamy vanes and the mind has fun on Queer Street. My annual rereading in the Christmas Octave is always instinctively the same: Conrad, Conan Doyle, W. W. Jacobs, Leonard Merrick, George Gissing, and C. J. Cutcliffe Hyne. These dreams are

[1]Copyright, 1949, by Duschnes Crawford, Inc.
[2]*Memoirs and Letters*, p. 91. University of Minnesota Press, 1934.
[3]*The New R.M.S. Caronia*, Cunard White Star booklet, 1949.

rubricated with flushes of innocent bibliography. I see myself
in a bookstore, say about 1903, and scream with mirth at the
embarrassment of the Trade (and the authors) when they find
that without warning two books have been almost simultaneously published so ridiculously confusable as Conrad: *Youth*,
and *Conrad in Quest of His Youth*. That alone is enough to
keep me happy until I wake, when I reflect how grim Mr. Conrad must have been if he noticed that Mr. Merrick was never
quite sure what is a taffrail.[4]

But this time I was dreaming the dream called Belonging to
Clubs. What put it into my turbines must have been talking to
a distinguished man of affairs who was offering the hospitality
of his own club for a literary dining-group that needed a room
for decorous assembly. Actually it was the Baker Street Irregulars, who carry bibliography to the verge of anaesthesia.
My friend found the steward of his club (the Marrow &
Squash) rather cagey. The steward wished to know, were the
proposed visitors really mature? The club had catered a dinner
for some young Wall Street men, where furniture and epithets
were thrown and $400 damage done to fine old English linen-
fold panelling.

My friend was appalled. He explained that the coterie he
sponsored were (was) a sodality of middle-aged Victorian lit-
terateurs. Most of them practically *are* old English panelling.
But I remember (from my days about town) that the Marrow
& Squash has (have) to be careful. I knew one of their members
whom they didn't like to wash out because he came of ten
lineal offsprings of Harvard (some of them badly sprung), but
he was only allowed inside the club as far as the cloak room
(left of the lobby) and the steward's desk where he could buy

[4]See *When Love Flies Out o' the Window*, and *One Man's View*.

(for cash) the club tie. Even that he gave up, because people thought it meant (red and blue) the University of Pennsylvania. He also gave up oldfashioneds, and now he is in *Who's Who in America* and *Bartlett's Quotations.*

I used to think (this is what I was laughing about) how wonderful it must be to belong to a Club. When I was 26—you can guess when that was—my dear old friend A. Edward (Amenity) Newton, as kind as wealthy, decided I should join a famous club of great collectors. You bibliophiles know the De Vinne Club. It has about 500 members, the most princely paramours of print and champagne in the western hemisphere. According to A. Edward they had decided they wanted a Baby Member, but among the engraved protocol they forgot it might be embarrassing to the nominee. Walter Gilliss, bless his old heart, was also a mover in the matter. Walter was so pleased by my having not only praised but memorized his inscription for the Printers' Sundial at Country Life Press,[5] it never occurred to the saintly old celibate that a young man complete with family might not only wear purple patches in his prose but also in his pants. As Bob Holliday and I used to say to each other, Where breek meets breek, there comes the tug of war.

The very day our first child was born, and I was digging like a dachshund in a badger-den, came the accolade, and a bill for initiation.

The honor (honour) of Letters, of Oxford, and even of Eddie Newton, was at stake. I borrowed money on the Morris (it should have been William Morris) Plan, and stalled doctor and hospital and nurse as long as I could. Soon, full of pride and

[5]"May thy unerring finger ever point
To those who printed first the written word."
See footnote, p. 1053, *Bartlett*, 12th edition.

terror, I went to one of those Sunday Night Suppers that were famous and cathartic at the De Vinne Club. Those meetings were Big Rubric and entirely democratic: all you had to do was bring one of your own most precious *ex libris carissimis* and give it a terse collation to the assembled Lorenzoes. It might be a quarto Hamlet, or a Songs of Innocence in unique color, even a Breeches Bible or some unbreeched Ben Franklin. I sat, *scelerisque purus*, between J. P. Morgan and Owen D. Young. The only rarissima I had on me was the final punch of a ten-trip ticket to Queens Village, L. I.

As a matter of fact I made very good friends with Mr. Morgan; he had forgotten his tobacco pouch, and borrowed some of my *Serene Mixture*. His pipe had a very large bowl, I remember. I used to see him sometimes afterward, on the L.I. train, and he remembered me as the man who had mild tobacco. He was pleased that my only other convert to that blend was dear old Hilaire Belloc. I used to say to him, it's like my books, it has never been advertised; and he replied Morgan's don't advertise either.

But I don't think the De Vinne Club has had a Baby Member since. As soon as my initiation fee expired I did also. I went there once, 30 years later, to see an exhibition of Max Beerbohm. I am sure that though the members know Max is a satirist they don't quite know what he is satirizing.

I moved, slightly foxed and shaken, to Philadelphia; and again dear Eddie Newton got busy. I found myself a member of that delightfully clannish little tavern on South Camac Street, and I don't mean the Poor Richard. There were only 100 members, but almost every one had written a book on Our Colonial Heritage. Therefore they didn't speak to each other, but only to me; and at length. Still (1949; it is my only social triumph) you will find over the hearth at the Philmagundi a church-warden clay that, reluctantly, I was forced to smoke at a fire of prerevolutionary billets. It is a sweet old club; nothing should be allowed to disturb it; nothing will. I wrote a book about Philadelphia (long before poor *Kitty Foyle*) which I had no heritage to do, and fled.

I got back to New York, two hours later, and Don Marquis said I must join The Mummers. That was a club of actors and writers and collectors and boblishers. They played pool, in the basement; once a week they had curried mutton and some delicious new wisecrack by Oliver Herford. It was difficult, though, for a young member, because the sibboleth was you mustn't say anything about plays or actors or writers because almost any other member might be implicated. I had always dreamed that a Club was where you could drop in about dusk (which comes early in winter) and after a Hard Day at the Office (if you could find an office) knock back a few at the bar, tell the agreeable Nubian at the phone to call the Little Woman (who seemed to get bigger as hours went by) and sit down to a sidetable under nineteenth-century playbills, and alongside nineteenth-century actors. You could sign the check for someone else's drinks, and lounge in professional gossip. But the inscription over the hearth expressly forbade gossip (which is the germ of creation) and even dear old Edwin Booth had been thrombosed by one of the very mild but agreeable verses of Tom Aldrich. The book was still open at the fatal page, in his bedroom upstairs.[6]

I never had the nerve to ask the Nubian to phone Long Island. If I didn't get home, say by 7 P.M., to put the furnace to bed, and help wash the dishes and the baby, who would?

[6]*Poems of T. B. Aldrich.* Houghton Mifflin & Co., 1882.

Came the horrors of 1929–30. I would have liked to go to The Mummers, but I was managing a theatre, and the Club was full of actors out of work, and managers out of angels. One could always buy an apple on a street-corner, and eat it in the Club, which was warm; even sometimes carve a drink out of a publisher, but according to the laws as by Edwin Booth and Mark Twain laid down you mustn't talk critical shop in the clubhouse. I resigned, just one two-cent stamp ahead of the Treasurer. But dear old Don Marquis, who had been my sponsor in 1920, was then chairman of the committee. "We can't possibly accept your resignation," he said. "Just carry on and forget about it." I did; I had plenty to carry, including what was then known as the Decline and Fall of the Hoboken Empire. I still remember (and would like to have the clipping buried with me) an editorial in the New York *Sun* which said the only bankruptcy it ever sentimentally regretted was that of the Hoboken theatres. The *Sun's* politics never moved me much, but its instinct toward the arts was always "Soyez gentil avec."

(What a genial topic, by the way, for a COLOPHON essay: the Attitudes of Various Papers toward Literature. I have seen, for instance, in 35 years, so many zigs and zags in the New York *Times* in book criticism that I don't know what not to believe. As Simeon Strunsky once said to me, the only subjects he felt were absolutely safe to praise in his then Topics of the Times were Sherlock Holmes, or Walking to Work (which John Finley had consecrated).

But à propos that Club in Gramercy Park. Fifteen years after resigning I had a notion to give it a MS, in honor of affectionate memories. It is now framed (they contributed the frame) near the bar; a letter written by F.D.R. about Don Marquis. I sent it, by a trusty hand, as a gift to the Club. They wrote: "We are delighted to have your gift; but we remind you, your name is still on the books and you owe the Club $250" (or something like that).

I must be brief, and very likely you also. There was the dignified Centipedes Club. One day of 1920, in the doublahvay of the *Evening Post* (there may be still in N.Y. a couple of hundred people who remember when New York had an evening paper that was liberal, literate, and lepid), dear old Sandy Noyes (the financial editor) told me they wanted a Baby Member. They had scanned their lists and found they had no one under Fifty. (I was then 30.) Even Henry Canby, Van Wyck Brooks, Elmer Davis, Leonard Bacon, and John Marquand weren't babyish enough for what they wanted. They wanted someone who would amuse Major Putnam, Henry Holt, and Nick Butler, without always contradicting them. My sponsor was that enchanting octogene Will H. Low, who had been a member for 50 years.[7] With a taxi driver I carried Will in to the meeting, on a tripos of canes. I saw I was about to be elected, and resigned at once. I was beginning to learn. Nothing gives me more malice and delight than when Henry Canby, or other much later members of that Club, ask me if I wouldn't be thrilled if they would Put Me Up.

I knew by then (say 1921) that clubs weren't for me, unless I invented them myself. I was quite happy, for a while, at dear old Frank Crowninshield's Café Noir on 45th Street, but if you didn't write for, or talk like, his *Vanity Fair*, you were gently eased out. Even Thackeray would have been greyballed.

I had to invent the Three Hours for Lunch Club, which existed only one meal at a time. We found ourselves owners of

[7] Have you read his delightful *Chronicle of Friendships?* Scribner, 1908.

a full-rigged sailing ship, *Tusitala*. Something had to be done about that. Then we invented The Foundry, in the ruins of an old ironworks in Hoboken. We had a gorgeous suite of Chinese Chippendale furniture in the skeleton of an abandoned machine-shop, with several residual blondes in the attic. In a few months, and after many impromptu lyrics in the old engine-room crank-pit, we found ourselves putative owners of some lithographed stock-paper, a contract for a Night Club, and a traffic in canned Mulligan. Something had to be done, and I had to do it. You'd be surprised to learn how intricate are the laws of New Jersey for Amicable Receivership. The canned soup of Eire was for a while transferred to the East 50's of Manhattan, where our business manager alternated singing "Mother Machree" and soliciting stock subscriptions; but even that, in the desiccations of 1931, blew away. Yet there are still occasional bohemians who remind me of the mixture of Irish sentiment and Irish bacon.

And still, poor soul, I had this morbid hanker for inventing clubs. Surely the most innocent impulse of my life was my boy-ish passion for the corn of Conan Doyle. I invented something called the Baker Street Irregulars; a simple group of a dozen devotees who met, Dutch, to discuss what amused them. It was taken up by that resonant soundingboard Woollcott, and then by *Life* magazine. The quiet speakeasy where we met was trampled into covercharge by runners and readers and their dames. Our scrapbook of minutes was stolen by some biblio-klept; our simple punchinello (Christ Cella) died of ambitious hypertension. Truly, men in Clubs have an urge toward Deficit, Damnation, and Death. Now the scholarly group of Baker Street find themselves swaddled, or saddled, with a publishing business, an annual meeting, and a province of pulp. They have about 30 scionist branches whose letters have to be answered. But not by me.

So you mustn't wonder that I found myself shocked, some dozen years ago, at being elected to the National Institute of Arts and Letters. I have never attended a meeting. I have a horror it might turn out to be a Club.

One has one's weaknesses. When I was last in London I was thrilled to see the fine old Athenaeum being repainted, a dazzling oyster-white, Elgin frieze and all. I did have a curiosity to know who now has hat-peg number 33 (which was Kipling's) or whether Henry Canby's order for iced-tea (which horrified the steward) has ever been repeated. I bet in there you could say what you think about acting, or editing, if you could get anybody to talk to you. The Savile and the Garrick must also be pleasant memberships. My friend James Whitall still yammers about the crumpets at the Savile; I think of it as the place where conscientious old Sidney Colvin was so excited to meet R.L.S. unexpectedly that he forgot a portfolio of valuable Italian drawings (belonging to the British Museum) and left them in the cab and they disappeared.[8] At the Garrick, as Baby Guest, I had the excitement of sitting at dinner between J. M. Barrie and Anthony Hope; our host was E. V. Lucas. But that was as foreigner and guest, which is the thing to be. I am proud to be an honorary member of the Omar Khayyam Club, partly because its annual dinner was poor George Gissing's only social jamboree. Gissing's usual instincts were far from festive. I love to remember that when he first went to Paris one of his earliest pilgrimages was to the Morgue.[9]

[8]See that most delightful of *meminisse juvabits*, Sir Edward Marsh's *A Number of People*. 1939.

[9]*Letters of George Gissing*, p. 177. Constable, 1927.

There are two clubs in London that not even their own members know apart. One is the Oxford and Cambridge, and the other the United Varsities. I have visited both, as a guest. I was agitated when in the coffee room of one or other my host (a cousin of mine, well over six feet six and well over sixty) said, "You're a varsity man, you should let me Put You Up, we need fresh blood." Next to us, at a lovely Queen Anne breakfront desk (they have lovely replicas of it at Abraham & Straus for $124.89), was an elderly parson making notes from a hidebound quarto and smoking a pipe and sipping a quarto of pale socialized India Ale.

The immortal story on this theme is of course James Bone's, done with his perfect concinnity in two lines:—

> "Drive me to the Caledonian Club."
> The taxi-man's face fell.

It was a shock to me when I realized I am not by temperament a clubman. It looks well in obits. But generally speaking (as I am) I prefer them vast and impersonal (like the Book-of-the-Month Club) or unsociable and imaginary, like the Diogenes Club where Mycroft spent every afternoon from 4.45 to 7.40.[10]

There was a club once (about 33 years ago) that had only two members. To them I dedicate this feeble echo of a laughing dream. It was the Porrier's Corner Club, near Doubleday's press on Long Island. It was a saloon where Robert Cortes Holliday[11] and I used to have a shell of beer (we could afford only one apiece) on our way home from work. We used to

[10]*Memoirs of Sherlock Holmes:* "The Greek Interpreter."

[11]He was then putting together his delightful collection of *Walking-Stick Papers.*

talk about Literature, which we loved and in our humble ways ensued. We talked about George Gissing and Richard Jefferies, about Don Marquis and Simeon Strunsky, and all the gorgeous things young men in publishing houses talk about. We would hammer the bar as we intoned our favorite war-cry, *I was a great solitary in my youth* (we always misquoted it).[12] One day an old man, I bet he was over fifty, who had been watching our antics, doddered up to us and said, "What do you boys talk about all the time? The Death of the Essay?"

"Mister," we cried, "them's fighting words."

[12]Stevenson: *The Pavilion on the Links.*

Notes on an Island[1]

I. GENERAL INFERENCE

IT WAS A WARM AUTUMN SATURDAY, BREEZY AND BRIGHT, as the train came down across the Midlands, from Liverpool to Euston. A visitor who has been so long away (seventeen years, and what years) looks close indeed to try to discern what has happened. Field and hedge, locomotive and signal box, cattle and cathedral, all had been through long mortal storm. On the sidings were strings of those gnomelike little goods wagons, each on four spindly wheels with spokes. It is easy to tell, by the spokes, whether the wagons are moving. Not nearly enough of them were. I saw with apprehension that many were filled with turnips and cabbage. The turnips, however, were "swedes," for fodder.

The visitor looks as sharp as a housewife. In back yards the family washing everywhere fluttered, to get the last of the week's air and sun. Washed and washed again, those humble

---

[1]Copyright, 1948, by Saturday Review Associates, Inc.

shirts and linens, heroic trivialities of our human woe—and all a dull cloudy oystery gray. England has little soap. I felt ashamed that I had hooked only one small cake from the C.P.R.

England has little soap; not even Soft Soap, for herself or for others. She must get very weary of being praised for stoicism, a tiresome virtue. Like everyone else she would prefer to be loved for what she feels in her heart: frivolity, mischief, and acute artistic sense. It is dangerous to try to make fair report because words in print are often given more heed than they merit. Even when you know a writer is a natural ass there is some wickedness in ink that lends him respect.

It would be easy to answer all questions by saying "A bit grim," because that is obviously what one is expected to say. But, for a traveller like me, England is still astonishingly comfortable. She has relaxed to my own social level; a shabby man can go almost anywhere without embarrassment. I was startled at first, then rather tickled, to see such proletarian figures trotting in and out of the offices in Whitehall. The black Homburg is still emblem of the professions, but would readily be doffed for a platter of Hamburg. I think I was a bit too jocular in chat with Lady—— at an Imperial soirée. She said, "I'm afraid you find us very down-at-heel." I said, "I like it. When your heels were high you had such a habit of putting them on people's necks." That was perhaps less than tactful in an Old Treacle Hand. But I did have a distinct impression in England that no one's boot is on anyone's nape—except of course Economics, which has its heel on us all.

Do not, therefore, say anything that might discourage the tourist. The American's inherited and infatuated curiosity about Britain, his mingled shock and delight when he puts it to proof, are among the island's greatest assets. His innate query is, What is it she has that we haven't got? She has plenty, including beauty that took time, good humor with a very high boiling point, and her unshaken habit of doing things, or not doing them, her own way. The North American, the world's great Handy Man, is in for many a shudder. A Canadian on the boat train, getting his first look at rolling stock, was baffled by all the little "wagons" shrouded with tarpaulin. "What have they got under all those canvases?" he exclaimed. "Corpses?"

It did seem like it, for a while. The corpse of transportation. Commerce was definitely at pause. The spokes of the little "mineral wagons" weren't spinning. The miners hadn't made up their minds whether to dig or not; nor do I blame them. I know what it feels like to sit down to a typewriter. But one of the first places I visited was Keats's house at Hampstead; and there, behind the mulberry tree where the nightingale ode was written, was a great dump of coal, unloaded in the garden. It was the same everywhere: whatever coal you could get hold of you piled in the garden, or the scullery, or the bowling green, or cloister. That, I said to myself, is England. Remember and revere the nightingale and the poet, but pile up the coal while you can. Elfland—with a Weather Eye.

The weather was unusual; it usually is. British meteorologists have learned not to make Forecasts. They print only what they call a General Inference. But weather seemed loath to bedevil the hardy island further, except with drouth. Tepid Saint Martin went on and on; Hyde Park orators were able to talk off distemper until late November.[2] The Labor Government

[2]How I wish someone would reread the tragic John Davidson's poem about Indian summer and railway stations (in London)—in his *Fleet Street* (1909; Mitchell Kennerley).

was combing thorns out of its hide. Like Br'er Rabbit, it was born and bred in a briar patch; it inherited a skinful of prickly problems, and invented new prickles of its own. Little Mr. Attlee's shanks didn't look comfortable propped on the table in the House of Commons. As you know, the Front Benchers show themselves at ease by hoisting their feet on the table. Perhaps the new tables in the House are not quite as wide as those that were blitzed? At any rate the reach is too far; I could see, from my perch (in the tiny balcony intended for Dominion Premiers), that Mr. Attlee had to sit quite on the bottom of his neck to make cantilever. It is an attitude that recalled the phrase that puzzled me as a schoolboy: the Rump Parliament. Mr. Churchill is too thick and too veteran to attempt it. Besides, you can't *lower* (lour) from that posture.

Mr. Eden, deliciously trim and self-aware, can look threatening even while he lolls. He has crural advantage; they are better striped, more debonair. He has his ankles to windward (on the Table) and his mind on the decimal system, whose address is Number Ten, Downing Street.

I must try not to be cheerful. It is fatal for an historian to think too much about things that amuse him.

Golden pause went on and on. It was like the *Ode to Autumn,* with its wonderful line that a boy in Philadelphia thought meant John Wanamaker: "Who hath not seen thee oft amid thy Store?" England was like Sleeping Beauty, stupefied within her quickset hedge, waiting for the cold accipitrine kiss of Sir Stafford. But the island is wary even in swoon. When she opens Parliament, or marries an Heir, she still makes Royalty ride in a glass coach, to be sure there's no deception. A new budget hung, like thunder on the left, over everyone's horizon. (Alas, poor Dalton, who fused his electricity betimes and

33

grounded thunder in the lobby.) Cigarettes were sold, when you could get them, in demi-pack of ten, including such un-kenned brands as "Fifth Avenue." (But there are actually two Fifth Avenues in London: one in Paddington, and one in East Ham.) Streets were dark at night; petrol perished. When you saw old U. S. Army trucks (as you often did) they were placarded behind: "Left Hand Drive: No Signal." That seemed to me a sort of emblem of the Socialist Government. With which, let me say, I am greatly in sympathy; but its psychological élan has been feeble. During my brief stay in England they sprang upon their glooming public two un-cushioned shocks, with no warning: Guy Faux petards under two of England's most revered bulwarks: the House of Lords and the Home Fleet. England was just as much shocked to learn how her Navy had shrunk as we are how ours has grown.

So everyone in England felt like a patient in the dentist's waiting room, reading an old copy of *Punch*. Even lovers of Moby Dick couldn't work up much zest for Antarctic Filet or Esquimaux Cutlet, which were caterers' names for whale; also called whaleburger. Drouth went on, douce but damnable. Farmers' fields were powder. Great cities like Manchester were within twelve days of water famine. English railways, usually the most exact in the world, had disastrous accidents, by fatigue and man-shortage. This was appalling to an American, who always loved English railways as the supreme example of toy trains: he wants to sprawl on the floor and play with them. Even before St. Paul's or Westminster Abbey the Ameri-can revisits all the old stygian stations. Pseudo-classic (Euston) or pseudo-gothic (St. Pancras) or pseudo-Bankofengland (L'pool Street) they harbor in their gloomy and agglomerated sheds more pressures of human emotion than any cathedrals.

I even did what relatively few English have done, took train (in a day of fog) from old Marylebone Station. That is a runway of mortal oddity that the Black Prince, or the Prince of Blackness, would relish. My old friend—dead these many years—Archie Macdonell—used it as starting point for his idyll of English oddity. Archie was a Scot, and the Scot comes near the American in his pawky sense of England's comedy of weird.

The Island was in trance. So was I; I could tell it by my sense of enjoyment and uncouth hilarity. My visit had double purpose: I wanted to see my English grandchild (I walked her in her pram up and down Sloane Street and round Lowndes Square) but I also wanted to see England, my grandmother. I had no prejudice in favor of either. England is about the same age as a nation as I am as a person. It is better for us both to take things easier than we have. England's wise and strategic inpulling of horns (or heels) is like my own. Life, whether of animals or nations, has its limitations. Events are going to move faster, from now on, than either I or she can deal with alone. So I say to the old emboggled men who like to think they're running the world, turn it over to the Young Folks. They'll do better than the official elders. I have nothing against Marshall, nor Molotov, nor the universal mischief Malapropos, except that they're old and tired and deprived. They were never lyric poets, and have worked harder than men should. Put them to bed. I only wish Stassen weren't getting bald so fast. The shrewdest political and oecumenical comment of our lifetime was that of the great Dr. Osler—and how he was razzed for it—to chloroform ambitious men at forty. I know, and you know too, it is men over forty who make trouble.

I don't think it's my fault; but it's usually my fortune, to visit any different civilization just when it's holding its breath. That is always difficult for an American.

The sense of wonder is the most precious, maybe the most exhausting, of mortal emotions. It doesn't last long; man, the coward, prefers to wallow in the familiar and the habitual. There is always wisdom in old catchwords: Nine Days' Wonder. True, for about the Tenth Day one begins to adapt, to osmoze. By then you have lost the fine bouquet of surprise. You no longer gape nor gripe at Britain's unchangeable habits, not even her explanatory interpolation "D'you see?" at every pause of narrative. By the tenth day you have given up trying to get a glass of water at meals, or preventing the waiter from pouring coffee and hot milk simultaneously into your cup (spoiling them both). You have remembered by then the fundamental lesson in dealing with all traditional peoples: it hurts them more to do it your way than it would hurt you to do it theirs. So you put the salt in a little pile on the rim of your plate; never directly on the cabbage or fish to be salted. You don't ask what the fish is, it's turbot.[3] You may speak without offense of any architectural ruins of the War, but do not, in charity, remark the most painful ruin of all, the shards and rubble of the noble English Sausage. It is gone, and (as the

[3] As it was in that great masterpiece of mild Victorian humor, Burnand's *Happy Thoughts*. I spent much time in London trying to find a copy of *Happy Thoughts* for some young people; the rising generation in Britain has had no chance to study that classic portrait of a mind full of fog. One of my pleasant memories is of Mr. John Wilson, dean of the London book trade, running up and down ladders to try to find me a copy which he was sure lurked somewhere in Bumpus's famous shop. For advanced students, *Happy Thoughts* is a lifelong favorite of Max Beerbohm's.

Shakespeare monument in Westminster Abbey spells it) "left not a wreck behind." Take the mustard, let the sausage go. But remember, better than any mustard (as international condiment) are these little differences.

Turbot was somehow comic even in Gilbert and Sullivan: in *Pinafore*, you remember, "turbot is ambitious brill." If not turbot, it's bream, plaice, mullet, haddock, cod, kipper, or bloater; or pilchard; even sprat. If fish is phosphorus, as they used to say, Britain will shine in the dark for centuries to come. We stayed, forty-five happy days, in a delightful little hotel (unknown to Americans, except for one Confederate colonel who was there one night and fled the next morning because there was no interpreter) which was itself, all glass and porcelain and iridescent reflections, very like a fishbowl. It was like a lens, or speculum, or cystoscope, into the very bowels of Britain. There was even a young man there who wore a morning coat for breakfast, put on a gray topper, and took taxi for the Opening of Parliament. From the experienced way he tweezed the hairy vertebrae of his kipper from his gums, I believe he was an hereditary Lord.

It is excellent politics, I said to myself, that these legislators ride the London taxi, which can twirl on a dime and reverse itself in mid-traffic.

But wonder, or strangeness, doesn't endure. I dare say Adam and Eve began to think themselves acclimated in Eden by the tenth day. Probably Karl Marx, up in Hampstead, believed after a week and a half that he was getting the hang of Britain? I think of Marx because 1948 is the centennial of his earnest manifesto, the burthen of which was his anxiety about exploitation; he himself was busy exploiting British lodgings

37

to try to undo British habits. I also think of Marx because he and Keats lived (thirty years apart) in the same street in Hampstead. Marx's boarding house has some terrible stained-glass windows. But Keats, as Shelley implied, wrote stained glass windows.

In those blasted heaths of ruin east of St. Paul's I found stained glass for myself. England's quickening soil for flowers sprouts autumn asters and marigolds and michaelmas daisies, natural rock gardens, in the checkerboard of ruin, so it seems almost like a common land; clumps of yellow and blue autumn wave in chinks of rubble, as Conservatives of the Nineties used to knot the colors on their whips when they went coaching to elections. When the City was blasted it was mixed with ruins older still; it is hard to know what was St. Giles Cripplegate and what was the old Roman Wall. There, moseying round with H. M. Tomlinson (birthright master of East London), I dug two scraps of red and green glass (port and starboard lights for memory) from the brickheaps of St. Giles Cripplegate. They were from a shattered window that had cast colored light on Milton's burial and Cromwell's wedding. Then we went down by Limehouse, Stepney, Poplar, and the East India Docks; even to Blackwall Stairs, where so many first families of Virginia and Massachusetts felt the first stomach of the sea. The old greasy cobbles they trod are still there. Tommy remembers when he netted shrimps there as a boy, but the tide now swells black as Scotch treacle. Shrimps prefer clean water; the only one we saw was a little girl about to do a pilgrim plunge on the slimy ramp. We dragged her back, wiped her nose, and begged her to be wary.

"I can't imagine what you want to see all this for," old Tommy kept murmuring as we rode bus down Commercial

Road, among landscapes of damnation. Then he suddenly became showman. "You see that church," pointing to a skeleton of walls. "That's where my wife and I were married." A little farther, another pile of ruin. "That's where my father and mother were married." Somewhere down by Robin Hood Lane (which would have astounded Robin Hood), or maybe Tunnel Gardens, there were more hollows of broken brick. "That was where my grandmother climbed out of the bedroom window and eloped with a young Navy officer." And Tommy's own home in Croydon was wrecked by a buzzbomb. He lives now in Hammersmith, farther upstream than ever before, but still within tidemarks.

It begins to look, I said, as if the Nazis had something against you.

The things not said are often the truest. Tommy didn't say, and probably didn't even think, it was rash of him, long ago, to write a beautiful book called *All Our Yesterdays*. Where are they? But neither of us thought that; we were more interested, both of us, in having lately become grandfathers.

There was other stained glass too. I saw the fourteenth-century windows in the chapel of New College, Oxford, being put together, piece by piece, after wartime burial. They were shown, for the moment, as few have ever seen them, behind a temporary screen, so they transfuse (as intended) only northern light. That is the light historians write by. And there were moments tinctured with the heraldry of chance. The only time we had to take shelter from actual rain was at Westminster Abbey. We retreated, with others, into a closed side-portal (the North Porch) while an April shower (in November) was falling in crystal douche across the sanctuary. But only a few rods away, beyond the street, the sun was shining like Chaucer, and the statue of Abe Lincoln gilded in cheerful bronze, bright as a new penny.

While we're at Westminster, I was sorry to notice they were straightening the bent sword of Richard the Lionheart. That twisted glaive was one of the things I wanted to see. But they had Richard inside a scaffold, evidently fixing him up. Like Shirley (in his glorious hymn they sing in the Abbey when a King dies), I prefer a broken sword in the hand of a stark man. Even more I admire the "poor crooked scythe and spade." See, if you are curious, your "Oxford Book" ✕296. Best of all, in that strong poem, 300 years in print, is the "victor-victim." We know, and well, all victors are victims too.[4]

We were speaking of the Sense of Surprise. I've been home on Long Island long enough for that awareness to dull. "Then fades the glimmering landscape on the sight." I am no longer startled by the horror of New York commuting (worse than the electric trains from Victoria or Waterloo), or the high cardiac pressure of commercial radio, or the inordinate adipose of newspapers, or the reluctance of Congress to face anything at par. I even accept, after a few trips to Town, the draggletail look of women in the new ¾ length skirts. Then I think of how many reasons Britain has to be grateful. Little miniature newspapers that you can put half a dozen of them in your coat pocket. Wireless without hysteria; you can be told, in sober and literate barytone, what seems to be happening; even a Royal Nuptial doesn't elicit the pizzicato molto

[4]I have just remembered: walking through ruins with Tommy, he wanted me to send him Steve Benét's fine inscription for the East River Drive in N. Y. City (at E. 25th Street). In part, Tommy, here it is: "Beneath this East River Drive of the City of New York lie stones, brick, and rubble from the bombed City of Bristol. . . . These fragments that once were homes shall testify while men love freedom to the resolution and fortitude of the people of Britain." (1942)

40

troppo of some aspirin or toothpaste. England is still, in secret, an aristocracy, for the only way you can find out what people are really thinking is by reading the letters to *The Times* or the *Manchester Guardian;* and the only way you can get those papers is by theft or by someone on the list of subscribers going abroad. I was able to get a black-market *Times,* after many visits to the underground newsstand at Knightsbridge, because some regular subscriber went to South Africa. While he was away digging (or raising "ground-nuts"?) in the Witwatersrand, I was reading his paper; I learned about the autumn misbehavior of the chiff-chaff (a Warbler or Lesser Pettychap), and the cleansing of the paintings at the National Gallery, and the fact that the Archbishop of Canterbury isn't responsible for everything said about USSR by the Dean of Canterbury. I wanted greatly to write a Letter to *The Times,* but what was on my mind had nothing to do with birds, edible fungi, or church ritual, so I knew it was futile.

There were many things I'd like to have written to The Papers. I am a good traveller, for my naïveté is absolute and miscroscopic, but I can take up a good deal of space. I felt it more considerate to impose it on American paper, where pulp is lavish. Also I was having a happily selfish time just meditating it for myself. Some of the letters I wanted to write:

(1) Love and congratulation to the new *Caronia,* launched and christened on the Clyde, in mid-November, by Princess Elizabeth, with young Prince Philip standing by. I was horrified that none of the news stories said anything about the old *Caronia* (launched, I think, about 1904) which was for many years one of the happiest of Atlantic ships. I should guess that about half a million Americans went to and fro in her; I did myself ten times; I even dedicated a book to her once,

though a very small one. She looked rather like Lord Halifax, very long for her beam, with an expansion joint amidships to absorb strain. A good idea for all travellers. So I wanted to send her new daughter my love and blessing, and beg her builders to change their minds and give the new *Caronia* two funnels, like the old ship, and a real open fire in the smokeroom, not just electric glass nuggets; and old Nighters, the middle-watch steward. Then, if there had been space, I would have concluded with a meditation: that all kinds of international musing are futile. Unless you love both nations equally, your ideas are crude; and as soon as love enters anywhere, they're just personal fantasy. Yours, Sir, etc.

(2) My delight at finding that a Toilet Saloon was a place where I could get my beard trimmed; *viz.*, a barber. The one I found, on Duke Street (they call it Juke Street), does all the haircutting for Eton College. Like thirty-five years ago, they put you in a windsor chair (Windsor is close to Eton) and you don't even take your coat off. So the little snips of hair go on your coat instead of down your neck. It's what that good man John Wilson, dean of the London book trade, always says of Pearsall Smith: "the art of the snippet." While you are waiting your turn at the Hairdresser you can read, instead of *Life* and *Time*, the alumni journals of the Royal Lancers and the Queens Bays. I never felt myself so definitely a gentleman. Yours, Sir, etc.

(3) One gets, of course, the notion that all the street cleansers (that's their name) are Anzacs; they wear the wideawake (as we would say, Stetson) pinned up on one side. They look so gloomy, with their little pushprams, you suppose they are Macaulay's New Zealanders come to study the ruins of St. Paul's. (How near they came to being Nazi instead of New

Zealand.) But only an American, with his austere literary discipline, is likely to remember Macaulay. Yours, Sir, etc.

(4) The great Johnsonian discovery, made by my Scots son-in-law. We had long been stricken by Boswell's quotation (p. 50, Oxford Press edition) that Johnson, while at Pembroke College, was usually seen "lounging about the college gate." This gave a suggestion of otiose Etonian idleness. Not at all. We visited Johnson's old rooms (now occupied by an American Rhodes Scholar). They are on the stairway above the porter's lodge. So young Sam hung about the lodge because there was always a fire in the porter's grate, and he couldn't afford one in his room. I would have added a few words about my wonderful visit to the Warden of New College, his noble old fourteenth-century kitchen, the Adventure of the Carton of Chesterfields, and the coltsfoot leaves he was drying to use as tobacco; but there wasn't, and never will be, space. Yours, Sir, etc.

(5) The lovely lady who shared with us a television festival —I think Chaucer would have called it a *flyting*—at a place called Alexandra Palace. It interested me because my grandfather, who had some acuity as realtor, was creeping his way up that plateau from Muswell Hill, about 1868. But what I liked most was Mrs. Halliday's cry of artists' woe: "When you get used to television, the movies seem so huge and crude and vulgar." All my Lilliput blood rose in joy to that, and I would have wished to say to *The Times* or *M. G.:* "England is a television country. Leave her so." Yrs, etc.,

(6) You can see (if you're the kind of reader I like to think you are) why I didn't write these letters. I could have written a letter about Traffic in Oxford compared with Tranquillity in Cambridge; or the Lady with Big Blue Eyes in Berkshire

and her cry of anguish, as she showed us her great black shoat in the barnyard: "Piggy! Poor Dear Pig! He's been Taken Over by the Government. And we had him All Fattened for Christmas!" That was in a midland midden that might have been Puck of Pook's Hill. The English go on living their literature, without remembering it's literature. To you and me it's too often something on a shelf. I would have added a brief glimpse of the huge Bengal tiger reaching his bended paw under the bars for a scarlet joint of horse-beef, at the Regents Park Zoo. You get a very good lunch there, by the way, with plenty of macerated potatoes and turnips and thick-skinned Socialist sausage; because you get Children's Priority. In the Socialist State (which none of our American Socialists have ever encountered in reality, not even Norman Thomas) children and carnivores get First Pick. Yours, Sir, etc.

(7) Six letters would have wound up a week for *The Times* or the *M. G.*, but there might still be a seventh for the *Sunday Times* (a quite different sheet), to which literary and historical queries are mostly addressed. Here I think I would have dwelt on the Other Pair of Shanks. These were the cotton-stocking shins of Mr. Speaker, sitting on his throne as arbiter of the House of Commons. The Speaker, in grey wig, black robe, and breeks, has his own formality no less than Front Benchers. One leg, even if the hose wrinkle a little, must dandle over the other; by the vibration of the swinging silver-buckled slipper the student, or Dominion Premier, may guess the under-current of debate. Anxiously, as argument trends toward partisan rapids or stagnant riposte, one sees the slipper toss faster, hang looser and looser on the suspensive great toe. Suppose, thinks the Dominioneer, slipper should fall off? The whole of parliamentary decorum depends from one nervous phalange.

And what a severity of argument that day: the matter of the Chancellor of Exchequer's gaffe was in debate. The Prime Minister was frozen and terse. The Leader of the Opposition, Mr. Churchill, was all jowls and jalap. Then it became obviously a to-and-fro, a squabble; each side gambiting for party position. The best gambit was (properly) Mr. Speaker's wrinkled shank. Toe, and slipper, swung faster and faster. Mr. Speaker takes no sides but that of House Itself. Suddenly he rose. "I think the House cannot profitably discuss this matter further at the present time." I quote from memory only, but you can enlarge me in Hansard, who is still the carbon paper of British Raj. (November 17, 1947.) There was no razz and no squawk. The House, without further yapping, proceeded to the order of the day. That, I thought, was England; and so were Mr. Attlee and Mr. Churchill, bending double, almost on all fours (more difficult for Churchill), to exchange some parliamentary advertisement during debate; creeping together, across the frontier (two sword-blades wide, by tradition), to confer below the Speaker's line of clairvoyance. You have never seen legislatures (any of them) in action until you have watched Mr. Speaker. Implemented with his scratch wig and his wrinkling hose, he is the emblem of impartiality. Out you go, between Westminster Hall and Westminster Abbey, and hunt long for your cup of tea. Spend a few weeks in England and you'll take tea seriously, or take it anyhow. Yours, Sir, etc.

2. L FOR LEARNER

LONDON AND I WERE A GOOD DEAL ALONE TOGETHER; WE planned it that way. The ladies of my house had errands and

affairs of their own; except to revisit a few old friends I wanted
to listen and look, with gazing fed. Of a thousand glimpses
what can one choose to write down? Perhaps nowhere on
earth has man's imagination, the gyroscopic spider in his skull,
concentered so intricate a web. One no longer remembers, or
cares, which was fact and which fancy. One sees Holmes
and Watson as clearly in the ruins of Baker Street as Johnson
and Boswell (in diuretic urgency) skipping under the roaring
busses to that easement in mid-Fleet. Among small pilgrimages,
impulsive and random (one should dominate one's worships),
some of those best memorable were one way or another associated with that great foursome of London friendship. *Nil
Londinii a me alienum puto;* but I think there was a special
pleasure in finding that in all dearth of materials the Dictionary
House in Gough Square had been given priority. It was in
the workmen's hands, and not yet fully repaired, but the
shibboleth is "A. Edward Newton." Mention that name John-
sonissimus and Mrs. Phyllis Rowell, the curatrix, throws débris
aside. She might tell you how, during the savageries of the
blitz, her old mother lay dying in that house. In age and
weakness her mind had fused the Doctor and the Deity. Blast
and fire were all round them; the exhausted firemen were getting casual soup and sleep on the floors of the Johnson house.
A shocking explosion sounded near, and the dying woman
said to her daughter: "Don't worry, dear; Our Old Sam
won't let us down." The Dictionary House will be open again
this spring, in substance as it was, but with one cherished
addition; a beautiful little miniature carpenter shop fashioned
for Mrs. Rowell by volunteer fire brigadiers, in memory of
their welcome at the Johnson House in intervals from struggle. It is a delicious mimicry, with tiny figures, benches, and

tools, carved from chips and shavings. In that house, if anywhere, the visitor feels short of words; but he can hear the
Doctor saying: "Madam, this is the triumph of affection united
with dexterity."

Boswell would have had much pleasure in noting the neighbors who now have the proximate quarters: The Society of
Correctors of the Press. That is, I suppose, a trade union of
proofreaders. They are lucky that Johnson and Boswell are
no longer on duty. I like to think, by the way, that Bozzy,
in the blitz and the buzz, would have come down from bomb-
exempt Auchinleck to share Johnson's dangers; and it is not hard
to imagine the arguments Mrs. Boswell could have offered
against it.

The proper pilgrim does devoir also to the living. There
was an extraordinary shock to see, still posted in a stark and
fireblacked entry of Kings Bench Walk—in the ruins of the
Temple—the nameplate MR. JAMES BONE. J. B. himself, whom
the New York *Times* once called "the greatest Londoner
since Dr. Johnson," is retired to an abbacy (Abbot's Holt)
in Surrey. But not even the gold and russet of autumn landscape, nor the gold and russet prose of his proofsheets (I wonder what the Correctors of the Press make of his handwriting,
on the galleys of his forthcoming book about London?), keep
him very long on Tilford Common. Last Summer's drouth
encouraged a heath fire (brush fire, we would call it) and
everything was cinders to his very hedge. Only a miraculous
change of wind, and an American girl who was visiting Mr.
and Mrs. Bone and derring-did with the garden hose, saved
their house. Blitzed out of The Temple, and torpedoed into
the North Atlantic, Mr. Bone was only a few inflammable
feet of shrubbery from losing another home. "I'm glad we

47

didn't; it would have been thought careless." But every few days the black oilcloth gripsack (you can't buy leather in England; it's all for export) carries J. B.'s proofsheets and pyjamas up to Fleet Street, where he makes appointment with you at El Vino, last of the sacred pubs.

By James Bone's kindness, and Freddy Bain's, I was able to make the kind of revisit that means most, to the great old "locals" of London River. The Grapes on Limehouse Reach; The Anchor, where Bankside turns round into the Clink; The Angel at Rotherhithe. The Anchor needs perhaps special mention: it has been strongly buttressed with huge beams after a shaking in the blitz, and the tap marked GIN, that comes right out of the wall, no longer flows (gin is scarce); but the Barclay & Perkins brewery is just behind it, and Johnson's head is still on the beer bottles. Not only that, it is probably the only bar in London that Shakespeare may have drunk in, for The Globe was just behind it. It was rather grim to hear that The Anchor is to be demolished for the new vast Bankside Power House. But there are many kinds of power houses, and they have their various destinies. The Globe had a voltage that is not forgotten. Mrs. Ellen Moy will continue to make her admirably utility sandwiches as long as the house stands. If I were Harvard University, or the General Motors Corporation, I would buy and remove The Anchor and Ellen Moy (stone by stone and sandwich by sandwich) to somewhere in the States; to show the young and jejune what a pub should look like. Alas they couldn't take with it the loveliest of all London's vespasians, opposite the door of The Anchor. You look across the River to the greatest broadside of St. Paul's.

After a wonderful utility lunch (and that means cod, cabbage, and boiled potatoes, and Courage's Stout) at The Angel,

Rotherhithe, you go, like Pepys (15 June 1664), to Cherry Gardens pier; and by water, "singing finely." Pepys had his breaks, and made the most of them, but he never travelled, as I did, in Supt. Fallon's launch down river as far as Erith and back to Wapping. It was the course of the Pursuit of the Andaman Islander (in *The Sign of the Four*), and Supt. T. Fallon's fast cruiser (he is head of the Thames River Police) leaps from lump to lump of the stream. Tide runs faster, deeper, and bumpier in London River than any of the old boatmen's madrigals ever told us. Cherry Gardens, I'm sure, is as far downstream as Pepys or Nell Gwynne ever went. If you go in tidal rip as far as Doyle's "melancholy Plumstead Marshes," or further to Gravesend, where Conrad and Marlow used to anchor the yawl, you better be steady with guts. But there is no other way to get a notion of the Courage Stout, and the estuary ebb and flood, and the great web of power-grids, on which London is built.

The India Docks were a commercial appendectomy. You have to get below that twisted gut (the Isle of Dogs) to see the great glands and bowels of service. Docks and ships, chimneys and transmission lines, even the old tawny canvassed sailing barges luffing across, I shall remember them in the rolling heave of grey and green misty sparkle. "Plenty of power round here," said Superintendent Fallon, pointing out various pools of potential. "All we need is a little push from somewhere. It's mostly in the mind, isn't it?"

There was one of Thames's pale-ale-colored sunsets as we came up river. Against the patched old canvas of the barges their men were heaving at huge leeboards and tillers. I was reminded of the Admiralty Appraisal of the *Mayflower* in 1624, when she was beached (or broken up?). The document

49

is preserved in the old Quaker barn at Jordans, Bucks., where some of her timbers perhaps still exist. She had "a suite of sailes more than half worn." They had a right to be.

But the *Mayflower* inventory also listed "five anchors," good evidence of prudent seamanship. The same strong old flukes that first hooked Massachusetts bottom. The visitor in Britain will see plenty of things more than half worn, from shirt or collars to railway carriages; he will see enough evidences of disaster, endurance, and fatigue. But more astonishing is how little is really changed. The anchors of temperament are in good holding ground. The British have passed, in their gradual and casual way, through a political and economic shift that would stagger many a tycoon. But the instinctive attitudes are the same. Still the elderly ladies sit muffled in their ancient furs in the glazed hotel lounge, watching to see if you do anything they can identify as "typically American." Still the curly-haired butcher on Sloane Street (I used to watch him through the window) keeps his queue of jaded housewives amused by an incessant patter of cockney comedy. The utility classes of Britain are the most humorous on earth. They have to be; in their oystershell climate they need to secrete pearl-juice. I was wondering why, aboard the C.P.R. liner, the emigrating British flocked with solemn acceptance to a succession of the most appalling Hollywood movies. A man of science, on his way to North America to try to sell British induction coils or something, told me the lurking truth. "They're starved for sunlight and black shadows. They don't pay any attention to the picture for people or plot. They just want to see sunshine and sky." Quite an essay could be written, by the way, on the C.P.R.'s preparatory drill, by movies and magazines, to indoctrinate its British passengers in

50

the North American Way. It was a rough passage, but not even seasickness could discourage the infatuated Britons from those color pictures of ski trails and diving girls, or Bob Montgomery letting himself go as a Tough Guy (Bob Montgomery! who used to be a Collector of Max Beerbohm!) or the color advertisements in *The Magazine Women Believe In*. How many emigrating grandmothers I saw in the Saloon Lounge, trying hard.

But how, I said to myself 1,000 times, is one small, more-than-half-worn, confused and impure mind—vitiated by love, detachment, skepticism, and indolent habit—to match itself against so large and troubled a panorama? Who could come surgeon-clean? Love and inheritance are themselves fatal to precision. Toynbee or Santayana might perhaps make luminescent (what I call neon-platonist) generalities. I could find few for myself. But I did keep seeing, in London papers, a financial note that Middlewits were up. It took me some time to figure out that had something to do with the Witwatersrand and gold shares. I preferred to take it as a personal hint.

A wise man noted that minnows skip on a turning tide. My own private pantheism believes that minnow can be as testimonial as man; I suspect that the minnow believes it is his own shiny capering that causes the tide to turn. There were plenty of social minnows on the skip, but I was looking for Middlewits. To put it another way, I was listening for the "dialing tone," which the British telephone identifies as "a purring sound." (What is so lonely, so abject-looking, as the British "call-box," sequestered up some dark alley or under a plane tree in a leafy alcove; rectangular relief for the bedtime dog.) It was a pity to be able to get *The Times* so rarely, because it

51

is in Letters to *The Times* that the intelligentsia blow their top; as in the Fourth Editorial they apply the demulcent of Humor-for-the-Few—the kind of prune-and-prism chaffing that no one but Simeon Strunsky has done in America since, well since Washington Irving? Letters to *The Times* are the dialing tone, the purring (or griping) sound of things to come. They are good, sturdy British beefing. Their writers, I said to myself cackling, are old Soup Stock. And they have had to learn, as no American ever did, the lesson of brevity.

The student of civilizations lives by self-denial. In the terrifying baritone of Bill Stern, unconscious energumen of football (feet are the chosen triumph and symbol of the Anglo-Saxon), he gets "out of the huddle very quickly now." His own habituated preferences mean nothing. He has to record, and relish (if England is his curiosity for the moment), sponge-bags and bread-sauce, nannies and nappies, bathtubs too deep and whiskies too shallow. But as the ancient immortal saying had it, when the customer complained there was a fly in his whiskey; the barman replied, "That's all roight, sir; 'e won't drown; 'is feet are on the bottom." So are John Bull's, and J. B. Priestley's. I'd nominate Priestley as a thumping good Prime Minister —he has somewhat the same qualities as Churchill—except for his brave, blooming compulsion to grind his teeth in public. At the very moment when every well-meaning American was trying to help the slow-cosseted movement to kick in, Old Candid Jack informed us that all Americans are hysterical sheep; and New York the crass crabmeat of the world. A man from Yorkshire should look less suddenly on New York.

I am trying to say, a visitor (any visitor, anywhere) has to look for the simplest and humblest emblems. In the English crossword puzzles the clues are quite different from our own.

You won't find them by travelling in the *Queens*, and going direct to the Dorchester and the Savoy. You're more likely to twig them in London Transport, or what we in New York call (to British amazement) a Comprehensive Omnibus. It is not distance that separates people; it is being too close. The *Queen Mary-Dorchester* type of visitors is only a flying wedge of the U.S.A. bulling their way a few yards between guard and tackle. If I wanted a real social document I'd hire a man like Bill Stern to live in England, muzzled, for a year, and then report to the U.S. about British Sports. Or I'd hire a commuter from Surrey (under gag for conditioning) to compare the train service from Charing Cross or Victoria with that of the Long Island Railroad. I have seen Victoria on a night of hellish fog; at least they give the season-ticket-holders an empty train to sleep in.

Differences being so subtle, what would you regard as clues in the stunningly chequered crossword puzzle of American-English relatives? I had an amusing dream not long ago, in which by some accident of oblique view I saw a burlesk chorus capering above me; as they stripped and teased I could see their eyes from about course 145°. It was curious to see the actual jelly and bulge of the eye, glittered by the footlights and prominent sideways. My dream continued into sheer farce when a Hokinson matron (who was there as an umpire of public morale) was carried away with excitement and began tearing off her own clothes, to everyone's dismay, and curvetting in the aisle and a percentage of slip. I mention that only because if one doesn't record a dream one forgets to analyze it. What I'm getting at is the sidelong jelly of the eye; things seen in dream or chance. Those are partly clues, partly testament.

We are, as Matthew Arnold said, between two worlds: one dead, one powerless to be born. Arnold enjoyed ribbing the Americans, almost as much as Jack Priestley does; but he begat grandchildren who became highly useful and distinguished Americans. So, more than likely, will Mr. Priestley. From the jackstraws (spillikins) of tumbled memory let me hook out a few slivers.

The methodical good sense of the English. See the signs in country towns: *No Waiting on This Side on Odd Days*. Waiting means parking. The idea is, you park on alternate sides of the street on alternate days. Result, no shopkeeper is permanently hurt by constant car-parking in front of his shop.— And the noble simplicity of putting a large red sign on the bonnet (of the car) of any apprentice driver. L FOR LEARNER. That means, give him the benefit of anxiety—a wide berth.

The stark simplicity of British statement. Almost every day I went past the Royal Artillery Memorial at Hyde Park Corner; at last—and in great peril, dodging the horrors of cloverleaf traffic—I decided to see what was carved on the base of that dead man. He lies in bronze, covered with coat and helmet. When I last saw him a light pall of snow whitened his rest. He symbolizes 49,076 dead of the Royal Artillery Regiment in 1914–18. And the statement: "Here was a Royal Fellowship of Death." It is more than November snow that chills you as you hunt an opening to Knightsbridge among the teeming traffic.

Or would it be Oxford, seen again in snell windy weather— Oxford of the sweet dreaming gasometers—Oxford that, more lucky than any university except Yale, now finds itself only the Latin Quarter of a factory town; like a bishop in Birmingham. So it has something on which to grind its teeth. The traffic on

Corn and High is worse than New York's Holland Tunnel. But there, bicycled in pedalled pause, are the flocks of youth—held in leash a moment by some yokel policeman's arm—waiting for signal. The arm descends and they flit off like a flight of starlings, like a wing of airplanes, on their way to lectures by C. S. Lewis or Father D'Arcy. The bells of Oxford have been almost drowned by the lorries. You have to get inside a college quadrangle before you can remember Roger Bacon or Duns Scotus or Matthew Arnold. I went into the front quad at BNC, to try to remember how St. Mary's spire looked from there when they had bonfires (I was thinking of the surly and surrogatory Pater), but all I learned was the B.N.C. 3rd VIII had made a number of bumps; it was chalked on an entry. I wish there were space to tell you of New College: of dear old Rose, the housemaid at the Warden's lodgings, to whom I gave a can of Canadian beef-cum-mushrooms and said, "This is my calling card." She fluttered her kindly tickle-eye and said, "It will be very welcome, sir." I saw it, next day, in that last of England's fourteenth-century kitchens, surmounting itself in the oven with a great arch of austerity pastry; what we would call a Warden Pye.

Oxford was always a carfax (carrefour) of traffic. She breathes, from her stricken towers, the latest enchantments of Lord Nuffield. We stayed, of course, in the last of England's frostbitten inns, the blessed old Golden Cross. That was where Shakespeare stayed, en route to and fro The Globe. His sheets, thanks to Mistress Davenant, were I hope warmer than mine. Postponing those gelations, I sped down St. Aldate's to hear Great Tom (Magnus Thomas) toll his 101 strokes, at 9.5 P.M. I listened, waited, and no booming bronze. Imperious as any outworn scholar has right to be, I questioned the Porter (proper in his round hard hat). "Yes sir, quite right, sir, but we're still on Summer Time. Christ Church goes on Greenwich Time. Thank you, sir."

The ghost that Oxford has given up can still be found at Cambridge; the ghost of silence. Cambridge is still mute. In her Cavendish laboratories, or where the organ and choir winnow the cool autumn air alongside the chapel of King's, or where the tame hedgehog probes the back lawns of John's with his inquest snout, you can still find the space and silence of academe. Nowhere else, I think, in the world? When new modes of international argument are shown, they are likely to be fissioned from Cambridge. Because Cambridge is bedded in silence, and in unspoiled archways where you see a great swath of scarlet creeper, flung like a doctor of science gown across the grey shoulder of a college.

"Euston always does this to me," said a young woman (a daughter) trying to keep her face under control. You don't know Dark and Damp, Delay, Doubt and Despair, until you've seen a Boat or a Leave Train from what they call the Departure Platform. Worse still there was a posse of the Salvation Army seeing off one of their benevolent brigadiers; he was going out to Save Canada; when his adjutants hymned "God Be With You," etc., it was too terrible. We took it personal. I saw our young woman's face beginning to slip. In our carriage was a young dog emigrating to Canada; he moaned like Manfred. And the Xmas number of the *Illustrated London News,* said W. H. Smith's newsstand, wouldn't be published until tomorrow. I knew that was absurd, because I'd seen it all over town, but thought I wouldn't buy it until getting aboard the train. If you don't read the stories, and no one ever does, the noble color-printing is like prose by Churchill: full of beef and brandy and thrippenny bits.

Yes, a dark day; the first snow had fallen; visibility was low. The great yellow and white gonfalons were already up along the Mall, for the Royal Wedding tomorrow, but in November light they looked more jaundice than gold. Was this the beginning of Another Winter? The Midlands were white with too early snowfall. Mrs. Gaskell, I thought, would have to wear her pattens in Cranford. In the carriage with us was a handsome young R. N. lieutenant, who looked so astoundingly like Prince Philip that I wondered at first had the bridegroom weakened and fled out on his assignment?

Spending most of the long cold journey (as I always do) in the corridor, to study what things look like, I saw that the little spoky wagon-wheels were spinning again. Just in those last few days the Island had got off dead center. Wheels were turning. Chimneys were puffing smoke. Even in the restorong car there was a kind of valedictory nostalgia in turnips and turbot.

It was a long chilly ride. Who but a lover of railways would be moved to think this was one of the latest travels under the great name of the L.M.S. (which I first knew as the immortal L.N.W.R.) before they became National Railways. Even Toynbee, even Sir Stafford Cripps, couldn't have been more intensified to consider, we were among the very last patrons of Private Enterprise. Myself I care little about ownership; I don't much care who hatches the eggs if I can fertilize and lay them. That is the fun; the rest is paper work.

The train was cold; the customs shed was cold (you go through Outbound Customs as well as Inbound, in our new world of fisco-analysis); and when we climbed the snowy gangplank to the *Empress of Canada* we were shocked and shamed. Tea with meat sandwiches (delicious thin sheaves of Canadian rare beef); cheese, Eccles cakes, hot water, liquid soap, towels laundered in crisp hundreds on the washroom racks—what had we done to deserve them? I was horrified, and still am. And the piles of toast, of fresh rolls, the tables of ham and turkey and the slicing-master with his shaven blade to curl off such slabs of veal-and-ham and Melton Mowbray. What is there in a tide-tabled gangplank to warrant one's passage from less than enough to too much? I suppose it is somehow credited as "export." It is as silly, and as selfish, as all human history. The rich white-shining outbound ship stands high at her cold and sleety pier. You look through the glassed-in windows of the promenade and see the last fourgons of baggage loaded aboard by chilblained men; do you wonder why people wonder? As I saw the great platters of rolls and buns I thought of the little old lady in Cambridge, who brought to every meal her little paper bag of crusts, saved from the day before.

We had fixed our sailing date long before Elizabeth and Philip did. I was sorry it had to be the night before the Wedding; but how tickled they were at our little glass hotel because they still had time to sell our rooms to four royalists. I felt in my simple way that two people's wedding is their own affair. I had found some of the antenuptial and millinery details hard to take. The description of Elizabeth's cami-knickers (an exclusively British lingerie) fitted with "little kicks of frosty lace" gave me no comfort at all. I only hoped that she herself, poor soul, was not required to read the description of her bridal bedgown, in oyster silk. These were

58

all in those scurvy little afternoon penny papers, where England shows her peasant psyche worse than we do. England does it in four pages, and takes it seriously. We do it in sixty-four pages, and roar from laughter. As in Thomas Hardy, too much of anything, even butchery, becomes comic.

The *Empress* ran into bad weather as soon as she was over the bar. The next morning, beyond the Mull of Kintyre, we were plunging in a nice old North of Ireland swell. It was drizzle and dour; those who had wrestled up from their berths were blanketed and supine in deck chairs. Then the BBC came on. In their earnest mode, so much more effective than American hysterics, the reporters along the Mall, along Whitehall, in The Abbey, told us about it. Sturdy British matrons, prostrate with seasickness, rallied up from their rugs; wizened Indian colonels strode the scuppers to hear. We heard the cheer, the cry of the British folk. I am, I think, a faithful reporter. Balancing against the looward rail, I listened. There was something maenad in that cry. It was more than a salute to two bashful and earnest young people. It was the voice of a race that had long had nothing to cheer. It rose above privations and queues and cold beds. It rose above the stately unsteamed homes of England; above discomfort and dearth. It was strange to hear it there, in the grey-green stormy waters north of the islands, in their own approved element of struggle. The beautiful white ship, loaded with good hope, buried her bright nose in dark northern gale. The voices of the air, the yell of stubborn millions worn by patient endurance, were not identifiable even as men, women, or children. They were the cry of an enduring race. Coal, for the first time, was over target. Steel was on the up and up. Themselves, by themselves if needed, could get round Cape Stiff. Despair was never their cup of tea.

As I heard that mixed and diapason roar, I thought of their great alien spokesman, Joseph Conrad. (They will never be good spokesmen for themselves.)

"You were a good crowd," he said. "As good a crowd as ever fisted a heavy foresail . . . or gave back yell for yell to a westerly gale."

I thought of that, and walked forward, alone, to smell the western sea.

Time of Life[1]

"YOU OUGHT TO DO MORE WORK IN THE COMMUNITY GAR-
den," the neighbors said. "It's so good for you." Wyncote was
amused. Fortunately, being amused was a habit of his; but only
one of his many habits.

Things grew rank that year. It was a strange summer: day
after day of rain, fog, drizzle, and exhausting humidity. It was
caused by an obstinate Bermuda High, the newspapers said,
which kept the northern seaboard under a heavy blanket of
depression. The Weather Man called it "an air mass boundary
that shows little or no movement." Wyncote got curious and
bought a barometer; he was amused when the humidity needle
went clean off the scale, above 100 per cent. Radio crackled
with static. Men's minds crackled, too. The brain is just as delicate an instrument as a radio. That's why they have such
trouble in getting together.

Rain fell straight and solid, didn't even bother to comb it-self out into crystal thread; sluiced in cataract down ivy and rose-creepers, poured over windowsills. Thunder idled round and round but never broke loose. Steaming swathes of mist were followed by brief blazes of jaundiced sunshine, too yellow to dry anything. Flies and mosquitoes stayed indoors. Spiders were too smart to build their webs and looked haggard. There was mould on books and clothes. Wyncote's razor blades grew rusty in spite of vaseline. Mrs. Wyncote's little stock of cock-tail biscuits, kept in case the Jenkinses should drop in, collapsed into spongy crumble. Everyone was limp and peevish. The air mass got so heavy, commuters said, the trains could hardly push through the tunnel into town. The crispest seersucker went draggle before smart young Mrs. Jenkins could meet her friends for lunch at the Circus Room in a Fifth Avenue store. "Hon-estly," she said, "I looked so blowsy people mistook me for the clown." A long friendship was bitterly wrenched when Mrs. McLomond served the Jenkinses a hard-fought cheese soufflé and Mr. Jenkins thought it was Yorkshire pudding.

Electric irons short-circuited, and several wives were worse shocked than they had been for years. The village laundry couldn't get anything dry and put up a sign OUT SHOPPEN BACK WHEN. Cars that halted uphill couldn't start again, carburetors were so condensed with wet. The climate just lay around on the ground waiting for people to kick it. The Jenk-inses, people who would have had fun together in the Alps, bickered a good deal at sea level. When Mrs Jenkins brought home an armful of costly slick-paper milady-type fashion maga-zines, the rain poured through an open window and melted them into solid unopenable slabs. Mr. Jenkins roared with laughter and said that would never happen to his *Quarterly*

Journal of Embryology. Afterward he was sorry; because he was sure Mrs. Jenkins woke him up when he hadn't really been snoring.

Everything grew wild and tropical that July. But Wyncote continued to work in the garden. It was so good for him. He larded the earth like Falstaff, and wondered if it was wise to take so many salt tablets, but he liked the name on the label: Sodium Chlorate Dextrose. Dextrose, he presumed, meant turn to the right. He was allowed only the humblest jobs in the community farm because he was an agricultural nincompoop; humbly he muttered his way on all fours along endless rows of root-crop, rescuing baby carrots and beets and artichokes from upas jungles of weed. He mumbled asinine sayings to himself: "If I forget thee, Jerusalem artichoke, may my dextrose forget her cunning." Sometimes, blinded with sweat, brain gorged with blood from creeping posture, he would fall prone in a steaming furrow and cry, "A garden is a lovesome thing, God wot."

Sultry afternoons of glebe and tilth, he would see, through shortsighted sweat-brimmed eyes, dim shapes of other garden-ers at work. He wondered what they thought. His own wretched small-talk with himself was a despairing effort not to think. He knew too well, geotropic soul, whither his notions were plunging. A garden is a carnal place, God wot. Vegetables with their innocent and shameless forms, so divinely accidental yet so full of fleshly anatomy—he turned embarrassed eyes away from crotched carrots and buttocky melons and glandular egg-plant. In that hot and burgeon season what appalling vitality, what thrusting struggle to exist and bear and repeat. What animal attitudes in the demure women of his colleagues. They came, shirt-shorted, in the royal flush of afternoon, to glean for their household supper.

The parallel lines of a garden always put the mind in Rhyme. He saw an unconscious desirable creature incredibly crimped into soft slopes of leg. He resumed his task, happy with doggerel. Baby bye, hip and thigh, he sang to himself. They crouch and squat, they bend and sweat, devoted squaws to the vegetable cause, I bet they'd do almost any sin for the sake of sufficient vitamin. Then, in prose, he wondered if the whole patriotic community, now eating so much vitamin roughage for the first time, was excessive with germination? Were they all hypoed with corn-sugar and beet-iron and watercress riboflavin; the riotous carbohydrates of the parsnip, the pungent aphrodisiac of caraway, dill, and wild thyme?

Maybe he better lie down in the furrow and pretend to be fast asleep, like Little Boy Blue.

When observant men, particularly at a Time of Life, get down to earth and look at it, jeepers, what dread parable it shows. And beauty everywhere! The tiny blood-thread of the beet; the blue and scarlet blossoms of the low or lofty bean! Who but the beanpicker knows profusion and plenty? Even its names are provocation: White Marrowfat, Red Kidney, Kentucky Wonder. Suppose, he said madly to himself, suppose under a pleached alley of Kentucky Wonders I met a lady with bluegrass vowels of compassion? And the promiscuous groaning bees double-bed with basil or blue borage. The lady-bug panniered in red; the blonde potato beetle; the pubic tassel of the corn. No wonder there is such a catalogue of herbs and vegetables in the *Song Which Is Solomon's*. How frightfully dishonest, he griped, are the translators' chapter headings in the Song. How annoyed Solomon would be.

He retrieved his glasses, tied a spare handkerchief round his

head to absorb moisture, abated anxiety by moving off to chores
in other parts of the field. With filleted brow he looked rather
like Catullus or any Roman erotic poet. And when he had
pulled up and tightened his falling trousers (Mrs. Jenkins noticed) he was quite a picturesque figure. He dusted wood-ash
on the flannel leaves of eggplant (or aubergine), he sniffed
pungent over the tall spires of the encyclical onion. Afternoon,
which had been tense with heat and anguish, suddenly breathed
deep from some lung of sky. A clarifying breeze whittled dryly
in the edged blades of corn.

He had pretended to be pleased by all these primitive senses.
Actually he was appalled. Mirth was his poor only armor; it is
not to be trusted. Some of the other gardeners were jocular,
too. Stout vestrymen, they also knew Solomon well enough to
parody. "He sheweth himself through the lettuce," they cried
to each other among the Black-Seeded Simpson, or when Big
Boston failed to head. There were gags worse than this. But the
wise do not sneer at play upon words. Sometimes it averts play
upon thoughts.

Late by lack of sunshine, the corn wasn't ripe to pick. Perhaps that purified him. Wyncote went back, chastened, to his
line of duty. Meanwhile Mrs. Jenkins, riper than the corn, had
made progress. She was editing a parallel row. How lovely she
was. Soon they would meet; head-on, which is the worst of so
many human meetings. What should he say? Sprawling mod-
estly among the foliage, he hitched up his pants again. She
wouldn't need to, he thought bitterly; she had visible means of
support. Besides, pants were too generous a plural for the narrow clout she wore.

He had weeded his way over the hilltop, over the watershed,
and was on the downslope to the hollow he called the Slough of

Despond. There, in a sag between two breasts of land, rich wet alluvion simmered; weed and parasite and strange warty growth flourished. Inflammation of sun turned it to proliferous mire, cracked with scaly surface paste where purslane fought No Surrender with the virile rhubarb.

There also, behind the shabby tool-shed, the abominable compost pile exhaled steaming corruption. It stank. There, defying our effete and puny genes, Demon and Demiurge staked all for win, place, or show. Wyncote always dreaded his task in that gulf of genesis where, as he said (only to himself), Behind was Let Loose. It was planned for helots and horror. In its thick morass anything grew strong and deep.

Deracinating with haul and twist the rubbery inertia of purslane (Puzzly, his colleagues called it), he coached himself by quoting Keats, probably *Endymion,* something about pipy stems. He was ashamed that a man of 50 had to get help from a poet of only 25, but that was one of the nice things about Wyncote, he could still be ashamed. Not of what he had done, but of what he hadn't. He had been scared by civilization, but he hadn't been cancelled. He always braced himself for the Slough, because there he really fought.

I must keep myself strong for the Slough, he said (ridiculous!) as Mrs. Jenkins came nearer. He peered down the reeking slope, where a great hedge of wild-grown sumac and sassafras ended the community terrain. The poison sumac, always damnably precocious, already in July announced what no one wanted to know, serene and sweetheart autumn. Even in the month of Julius (also murdered early) the clear green sumac was tipped with scarlet chevrons, like noncom Marines. It was, as they say backstage, First Warning. Wyncote had had it too.

He and Mrs. Jenkins met, in echelon; he in the masculine crawl and she in the pelvic squat. There was nothing between them but a file of puritan Swiss chard. Her thighs shaded brown paling to ivory; her bosom depended in perfect mammal catenary. Her eyes were clear; his, bloodshot blear. She perspired sweet; he was foul with heat. They paused and looked hard, across the chard.

He read (he was a good reader) something anti-Jenkins in her gaze. Helvetian neutrality grows high and rugged, but they might have leaned across it. It would have been a delicious sweaty kiss, slippery-sweet, and no harm to anyone. But he was ruined by the Song of Solomon, which had been in his mind.

He wanted to say something about roes that are twins and was too bashful. So he said (and it's always a mistake to say your own thought instead of one of Solomon's), "I am the scapegoat of the Lord! I am the Vacuum Abhorred."

Quite rightly, she abhorred him. She went on weeding south; he went on weeding north. Once he stopped and looked back. She was graceful, though plumply grooved, from behind.

When he got down to the Slough he lay on his belly in the mud, gripping filthy purslane with both hands, and through the hedge he saw Cybele.

Cybele, whose family came from the re-sodded Pontine marshes, took sloughs as they came; she might have come from Catullus, or Ovid, or even Horace—any of the textbooks that the boys aren't supposed to take seriously, and fortunately don't. She lay in a hammock with her feet higher than her head, though Wyncote, looking through the hedge from below, noticed more hummock than hammock. She was reading a newspaper cartoon strip, and she was just as delicately shaded brown to gold to milky as Mrs. Jenkins, and just as bifurcated as any carrot. It is amazing how translucent a hedge can be if you look fiercely at it. Wyncote, leaving purslane to wrestle with rhubarb, crept like a Ranger toward the shrubbery and groped into it. Through the leaves, dripping the bronze of sunset, he gaped and prickled like a faun.

Unconscious Cybele swung softly to and fro, coolly ungirt in her cotton wrapper, moulding the thin hammock with fulnesses unrestrained. She was absorbed in *Terry and the Pirates*, regardless of worse piracy near by. The fecund Slough, cooking with creation, seemed to swing too. Wyncote lay there, caught in some horrid earth rhythm: pulsated, frustrated, ill-fated. Perhaps he blurted shameless petition to some furious lurking god.

Came August, hot, clear, and consummate: month of fruit and foreboding; month of grace exhausted and power leakage. Oh August, month of the golden beryl, season when restraint seems sterile, month of harvest, war, and peril; cooling dusk on the mounded hay, month nine months ahead of May. The August moon, first shrivelled and thin (like an empty vineyard skin), gently filled its bladder hollow with a glowing cider-yellow.

The conscientious gardeners of the parish, weary and tanned, met in their screened porches and put on again with beer and pretzels the adipose they had swinked off in the field. They made their little jokes, perhaps to drown out the sorry tinkle of the crickets who had suddenly tuned in. "*Lammas tide*," said the rector, who knew more about Anglican festivals than was quite seemly in a Republican, "Lammas, that means Loaf-Mass, to sanctify the harvest loaf."

"A good loaf is what I need," said poor Mr. Jenkins, who had been terribly pooped all summer.

"Lammas is quarter-day in Scotland," said Mr. McLomond. "Even the Scotch have to pay their rent."

They were all pleasant, cultivated people; the husbands rich in the varied lore of grizzled commuters and vestrymen; even the wives had almost all been through junior college and would bandy a highball or an allusion with anyone.

"I'm all for Yeats and seven beanoes," said Phoebe Jenkins, "but I can't swallow any more chard. There's a legume that really girds its loins for production."

"Chard is not a legume," Mr. Jenkins contradicted. "Legumes are pulse, viz., peas, beans, and lentils. Also Yeats had *nine* bean rows, not seven."

"Bilbo!" exclaimed Mrs. Jenkins. (This was a coinage of their own to express absolute rot.) "It makes me furious when you say *viz.* Academic jocularity."

Wyncote was glad anyhow that the conversation was not going to turn on loins. He stuffed a handful of salted peanuts to prevent himself from making a catalytic wisecrack about Sir Loin and Lady Loin.

They agreed to plant fewer greens next year. "By the way," said someone, "there's been complaint from folks down the road, Sibby Campagna and others. It seems the compost pile smells very strong this year."

Indeed it did. In that heat-fermenting hollow the great mass of stewing sirupy stuff exhaled a haze of fume and flies. It was nature joyriding toward corruption, an orgy of organisms redeploying.

Wyncote and the rector walked part way home together in

the chanting summer night. Beer, Wyncote thought sadly, was hardly a strong enough drink to muffle the Gregorian plainsong of the crickets. The rector, whose anxious profession it was to see that nothing anywhere got out from under decent wraps, remarked that the parish had been plagued lately with an almost hysterical barking of dogs.

"Dogs are such prudes," said Wyncote.

"No, but really; there has been an almost Hound of the Baskervilles baying among the woods. I wouldn't say this to everybody but it's quite ghastly, almost a human note in the dreadful yowling, like a woman in her agony, but awfully not quite."

"Maybe not Baskervilles, but Durbervilles."

"It's not even funny," reproached the parson, who had children in high school and was adept in their language. "And have you noticed the signs about mad dogs? We don't dare let our pooch out any more except on a leash. I have to prepare my sermons while I'm walking the dog, and sometimes I'm afraid I get too realistic."

No one ought to be let out except on a leash, thought Citizen Wyncote. Wisdom is better than rabies. But he felt it wise not to say anything further.

Because something was plainly wrong. It wasn't just the scandal-wail of dogs. Their trouble might have been the record multiplication of fleas in that humid weather. Each flea had to get along with a smaller section of dog, and so bit harder and faster. But everything was in excess. Japanese beetles, in disgusting pairs, tore open the pink linen of the rose. Moths, agnostic of crystal parabenzine, went nurseling in grocery cupboards. Flies were prodigal of their specks. Books swelled and bloated on the shelves so that reviewers couldn't look up quotations.

People spread and stuck to their seats in trains and were carried past the proper stations. Caravans of nervous ants, moving their larvae to dryer apartments, climbed what they thought were glossy white birch trees. They were legs; Mrs. Jenkins' and others less Duncan Phyfe. Bees, always shortsighted, got confused and cross-fertilized at random, so hydrangeas and phlox changed color. The hawthorn shed bald. Mrs. Jenkins piled her hair on top of her head to keep her nape cool.

Wyncote noticed all these phenomena, and stayed indoors. It was his business to notice things and not do anything about them. He had been busy all summer on a four-line epigram, which he planned to offer to a publisher for publication in 1948. So he was happy and absorbed, sitting X-legged by his bookshelves trying to pull out a copy of *The Golden Bough* that had mouldered tight against *Whitaker's Almanac*, when Jenkins came in. Wyncote got out a bottle and mixed a Rum Collins.

"Make it more rum than collins," said Jenkins sighing. "My wife's away visiting I need a night's sleep."

Wyncote wondered how that sentence was punctuated. Then he wished he could get over the habit of wondering about things that weren't comma unfortunately comma any of his affair.

They talked a while, as mannerly neighbors, about casual nothings. "I haven't got my fuel coupons yet," said Wyncote. "It's going to be a tough winter."

Kapellmeister crickets outside, rubbing their wiry shins, shrilled damning assent. How fortunate, Wyncote thought, people don't talk about what life is really like. They leave that to the compost piles and crickets. He noticed he had given Mr. Jenkins his drink in the toothglass with which he had been rinsing his retiring gums. How did it get out of the powder

71

room? At any rate, I haven't completely failed in life. I have a powder room.

"Let's not be morbid," he exclaimed, to keep the conversation going, as Jenkins looked very sombre. That was a wisecrack he often found useful when talk went sour.

"That's exactly what I am," said honest Jenkins. "Have you seen what's happened in the Garden?—Say, get me another drink, this one tastes like peroxide."

Wyncote felt guilty. He hadn't been down to the field lately, since the planting and weeding jobs were over.

Cheered by the fresh drink, Mr. Jenkins tried to explain. He was wary and waggish as a disciplined vestryman should be. He beat around the bush like the chapter headings in the Song. He spoke of the howling of dogs, the strange odors that drifted through that part of the woodland, shouts and screams that had been heard, apparently in a foreign language.

"How do you tell what language is a scream?" asked Wyncote.

Jenkins grew more detailed. Mrs. Jenkins was away and he began to feel the vigorous frankness of the husband whose wife is out of earshot. Wyncote feared he would have to hush him down, for Mrs. Wyncote, who had gone upstairs, might not be asleep. How husband-like, he thought. The old boy doesn't care whose wife overhears as long as his own doesn't.

"Phoebe was terribly upset," Mr. Jenkins was continuing. "She came back that night pale as a sheet. She swears she was chased."

"Chaste?" babbled Wyncote. "Why, of course. I never saw a more virtuous group of women anywhere."

"You fool, C-H-A-S-E-D. Chased down by the Copse."

The Copse, in the picturesque realtors' jargon of that section,

72

was the winding wood road that led past the community garden, but Wyncote still misunderstood.

Jenkins finished his glass. "All right, you think I'm inventing, come down with me and have a look. The moon's bright, and if you want to see something really bestial bring your flashlight. Mac and Bill and Steve and I have been watching it. I'm telling you, it's appalling, polluted, unspeakable, disgusting, and incredible. Bill says it looks like soandso, and Steve says suchandsuch, and Mac won't commit himself. Thank goodness, it's down in the Slough you're so fond of, below the beans and cucumbers, so we've kept the girls from seeing it up to now. But the way it's growing they're bound to notice. Bill says he don't dare call the usual harvest meeting, someone might mention it."

Moonlight is austere and sanative; a sort of cosmic peroxide. What might be abominable at 1500 hours can be sweet and commendable at 2300. What a difference eight hours make. The mass of sprawling cucumber vines, the long-cast tracery shadow of pole-beans (like a music score), the low demijohn moon, softened with merciful crisscross the Gruesome Thing, but certainly there was a foul smell, and a dark shape seemed to slip off behind the roadside trees. A dog near by began barking on its top terrified note.

"Maybe it's Bill's melons," suggested Wyncote as he slipped on a soft one. "He's too lazy to harvest them, and they always reek."

"Whatever it is, I take a dim view of it," said Jenkins.

Wyncote turned on his flashlight, and turned off again quickly. "A dim view is best," he said. Between decent earthy furrows was a disordered trampled area; and weltered and half revealed in steaming mire a strange suggestive growth.

"Certainly nothing to write home about," Wyncote said presently. "I see what you mean, but it doesn't look like that to me."

"And what do you think of these?" asked Jenkins, pointing to pairs of dark prints deeply sunk in the soft slope.

Wyncote did not hesitate to quote Old Testament to a vestryman. "Maybe the Daughter of Zion in a garden of cucumbers," he said.

"Appears to me somebody working in this garden had a mighty dirty mind," said Jenkins. "Somebody put a hex on some unconscious vegetable and turned it into a hellish symbol. I'm going to call a meeting next week, stag, without asking the girls to come, and see what can be done. It might be better just to have the older men. The young fellows are too gabby."

That was easy for Jenkins. His wife was away in the clean granite uplands of New Hampshire. The other women wanted to know why, for the first time in the history of democratic glebing, they were barred. Several of them were astonished at this time when their husbands offered them travellers' checks and a holiday with the children Upstate. But no woman accepts a holiday that someone else thinks up for her.

Several days of secret negotiation had to pass before the men could get together privately. Strange things were said in the brief moments when they met, pushing through the train in quest of seats, buying newpapers at the depot, or sneaking singly into the village liquor store. (None wished to know if his fellows had equal favor in the fluctuating supplies of Scotch and gin.)

"Everybody says, it don't look Like That to me," said Bill

when the Horrid Thing was mentioned. "They're hypocrites."

Mr. Jenkins wondered if maybe the rector could exorcise it with a ritual; he had read of that sort of thing in Conan Doyle. But the rector, shrewd man, chose that week to go on leave. Meanwhile, the Thing grew strong and sultry behind the cucumbers. Even Cybele must have noticed it, for her hammock lay empty, in flat suspense. The Augustan sun thickened the Slough to a curdled emulsion in which bubbles of gas rose and puked. Edged with putrid moss, the shape was still inchoate, formless, and therefore visible in all forms forbidden and obscene. The committee unloaded a truck of straw upon it, but even this harmless covering made slow quiver and heave.

It was the beginning of September, the very dark of the moon, when they met, like conspirators, at Jenkins' house to equip. The suggestion of engaging a plane from the Army, to drop a precision bomb, had been voted down. The story then would be out, and very damaging to real estate values. Wyncote, who felt a peculiar, but top-secret, responsibility, had procured the largest flame-throwing weed-killer on the market and a mask. The others brought rubber boots, pitchforks, sharpened spades, quicklime, lysol, anything they could think of. The women, of course, by now had a pretty good idea of what was going on, except that they visualized the Thing even worse (and quite different) from fact. They shut themselves in, with wax ear-stoppers and the loudest comedians they could find on the radio.

The weather broke that night. Perhaps it was the first of the September hurricanes. Just as well, for the thunder helped to cover those awful whinnying screams. The electrical convulsions were severe. Lights and telephone service went askew. Everyone got wrong numbers. Seen in terrifying flares of light-

75

ning, the Thing appeared to have taken on animal life as well as vegetable. It wallowed, groaned, and struggled, and a strange piping whistled in the wind-strained trees. The committee were all a little berserk; they had primed with strong drink and were surprised to find themselves shouting and singing wildly as they attacked. A frenzy possessed them; each seemed to identify this Unspeakable with whatever had troubled him worst in a hard life. They uttered names and cries mercifully never recalled. Wyncote, bawling some impromptu incantation, rushed in pumping the flame thrower; he sank waist-deep into the unholy Slough. Living rubber ropes of fighting purslane, or some other kind of vile tentacles, nearly dragged him under. They cut and slashed and slogged. Then the gassy flame poured on. There was a meaty cindering sizzle. Night split with screams, a great tree crashed across the road. Cybele and her kin, beyond the hedge, might well have wondered what hell was happening; but like all good Latins in thunder they were humped under the mattress telling beads.

There was silence, and relief, until the crickets resumed their methodical metronome dirge. Perhaps, mopping themselves, some of the gardeners felt that what had begun as a sanitary squad had ended as a murder gang. But man never really regrets anything that makes him sweat. They piled rocks on the place, trudged back the sylvestered way.

Mrs. Wyncote, completely foxed by the whole episode, had nightcaps ready for the men when they came back, drenched and mired and smelly. As usual, she thought, Mr. Wyncote smelled worst.

There were no ice cubes, because everything civilized in the house (even the powder room) had gone out of order. The barometer had gone up and down wildly. Perhaps that was why both Sheffield and Borden had so much trouble next day. The milk was very strong. Everyone said it tasted like goat's milk.

"What on earth was that you were shouting as you ran into the Slough?" asked Mr. Jenkins as they drank their last by candlelight. "You were yelling like crazy, something about *A dismal cry rose slowly, full of something melancholy, and something else despair.*"

Wyncote was too tired to be polite. "Was I? I didn't know. I guess it was Mrs. Browning's grand poem about poker."

"About poker? Surely not!"

"Probably I'm mixed up. Well, good night."

Labor Day came pure and cool. Mr. Jenkins forgot about the poem, but wrote to Phoebe telling her what a time they'd had fighting a flood at the Disposal Plant. In dryer air, books came unstuck; Wyncote pulled out Mrs. Browning and reread the poker poem—the one called *Dead Pan.*

Saint Bypass[1]

A CONSCIENTIOUS WAR DEPARTMENT, OR TRIUNIFIED SERVICE, thinks about things a long time ahead (I hope it's a long time). One of its anxieties is getting the populace (that's you and me) Out of Town when Disaster comes. Never mind what Town, never mind what Disaster. It had long been plain that commuting railroads and bus lines could hardly handle normal weekend escape. What would it be like when D-Day comes, the Great Dispersion?

Every Army, everywhere, knows that another war would be unwinnable by anyone. Curtains for all, and not even the humble posset of a curtain-lecture. But the Army is cool and consequential as an anthill. Its only concern is to figure out how a percentage can perhaps survive, pooped but unsterilized, and start all over again. Armies are tactful (until you get into them) but what they always have in mind is the coefficient of survival. Civilian survival.

[1]Copyright, 1947, by The Associated Magazines Contributors, Inc.

So they try to eliminate bottlenecks. One of the most in-
testinal constipations for outbound traffic from Vulnerable City
is the long narrow bending dip through Wending Ways, a
modest old bailiwick some twenty-five miles away. The Army
decided to short-circuit it. The local Lions Club roared, and the
Kiwanis Club resolved, and a couple of high-priced roadhouses
took most of the clams out of their chowder; but War has
Eminent Domain. Grinding slow but small (like the chowder-
chef), it condemned enough property to clear its Right of
Way. It plotted a huge viaduct across Wending Harbor. The
village, lingering in an acute angle of low tide and lethargy, was
cut out of arterial flow.

The great white viaduct was nerved with steel, fleshed with
concrete, hypothecated with taxpayers. Countenanced by Congress, guaranteed by the Governor (he never visits our county,
he gets 80 per cent of our vote by mesmerism), the noble
structure strode. Strode? I mean leaped, level and luminous
from hill to hill. The old sentimental village where William
Cullen Bryan, or William Jennings Bryant (I get confused,
myself), wrote *Thanatopsis,* or *The Cross of Gold,* was left
out on a limb.

Down in their anxious lagoon the citizens bubbled like frustrated frogs. Who, now, would drive down their picturesque
gully, where the antique furniture was all ready on the side-
walk, where the house waited in which Washington only had
breakfast and didn't spend the night? (He knew those corn-
shuck mattresses, and hastened on to the Astor House.) On the
high six-lane bridge, fit for the flight of a Tartar tribe, hell and
holiday went whickering by. Unless you were on the right-
hand strip, no one pushing your bumper, and had on your new
glasses (to read the minuscule sign: WENDING WAYS, *next right*

turn, 1000 feet), you couldn't divert to the deserted village. It was cut off, like a fecalith appendix.

All this time, and a long time before that, there was a patient little church in Wending Ways, dedicated to the holy hermit Saint Bypass. It stood on the far side of the village, just where the retorted turnpike has another crick in its bottleneck and climbs from the entrails of town toward the lungs of the eastern highland.

It was a beautiful church, one of those costly sanctuaries impulsively endowed by wealthy ladies who may have their own reasons for spiritual disturbance. The benefactress had hired a famous imitative architect and there was a lovely campanile of Tuscan brick. By some error in the casting cauldron the bronze bells rang just effably one semitone off true chime. In fact, there was long secular argument about that: The vestry and the lady's estate both maintained that payment should also be a grace note below pitch. With this divine demurrage hanging over them, and a retentive congregation, the vestry could never afford to stiffen up the pews (which were wabbly and swayback) or dig a cellar and fluent plumbing for the rectory.

It was a grave little church, very likely loved all the better by God for its human embarrassments. Nothing more impels Deity to sympathy and sufferance than man's inept gestures toward devotion. The church of Saint Bypass, set on an abrupt jog of uphill road, was built and beneficed in the very year when the horseless carriage was invented. It was planned and placed for that slow, wheel-sifting, sandy traffic when horse was hierarch. The first automobilist, in his demon gear of duster and goggles, was ill omen for Saint Bypass.

Soon there was no way to get to church (except for eight
o'clock matins) but by turning left across traffic. Even putting
a policeman at the turning didn't help; the cop naturally as-
sumed you wanted to go to the Other Church, which was always mandated full, and waved you down the side lane. A few
intending worshippers got so baffled they found themselves in
the Friends' Meeting House over at East Porridge. They were
afraid to go again, because the Friendly elders rushed out to
shake hands after the meeting. Some people find it hard to be
folksy just after prayer.

While the Army's great construction was proceeding, the
plight of Saint Bypass was grim. Long scalene limbs of cranes
waved above the modest belfry; roaring tractors, concrete
mixers, pile drivers, deafened the neighborhood. The rectory,
never too sturdy and perched on a slope, quaked like blanc-
mange. Wide cracks opened in the parson's consulting room.
"How unfirm a foundation," he said to himself. During those
thunderous weekdays the rector even attempted the trick of
Oriental rhapsodists, putting himself in trance by swallowing
his tongue. That member was no use to him anyway, he said,
since anything uttered was inaudible. But a tongue well and
truly swallowed is hard to regurge; once he only just got it
limbered in time to preach on Sunday.

A few loyal and hardy parishioners managed to clamber to
services through excavations and along dusty gangways. What
traffic was possible was mostly detoured by the Other Church,
still thriving and shriving. Army engineers with trigonometry
eyes had cased both sanctuaries and planned it that way. Some
of Saint Bypass' trusties went a little queer with congested

litany. One was found squatting under the noble old oak tree at the Friends' Meeting House. He had a salad bowl for small cash and said he was Buddha. They knew he wasn't a real mystic, however, because he couldn't sit cross-legged for more than half an hour without groaning.

But the rector was a man of spirit. While the church was practically inaccessible he always hummed hymn 177 (*Angels, roll the rock away*) and caught up on his parish visiting. He encouraged the subscription for a helicopter to pick up the zealous and land them on the small church lawn. With the giant viaduct straddling right over him, he got the Bishop's permission to enlarge the church's name to Saint Bypass-under-the-Bridge. He instanced Saint Mary-le-Bow, and the ecclesiastical Court of Arches. The name would have a romantic and historic appeal and might arouse worshipful curiosity. Like all good rectors, he was, when given a chance, a man of letters, and quoted Wordsworth: *Turn your necessity to glorious gain.*

Also, during this turmoil, he inclined his heart to reading and study. Among the properties condemned by the Army was the old village library, a delicious example of Currier and Ives Gothic, dripping with wooden stalactites. The older books, that no one had wanted to read for fifty years, had been bundled and stacked in the parish hall, and he had fun rediscovering such pleasing old writers as Mary Russell Mitford and *Annals of the Parish*, Ik Marvel and Jules Verne, Frank Stockton and F. Anstey.

He read the newspapers, which holy men are wiser not to do, but he was ironist enough to swallow his tongue when he read the headline WAR STRENGTH BY CHRISTMAS.[2] Maybe a good idea, he mused (while wiping the dust of powdered

[2]For the record: New York *Times*, page 1, July 26, 1947.

cement from altar and chancel) if some national spokesmen would swallow their tongues?

He also dusted his old *Bartlett*, the clergyman's privy counsellor, and looked up Matthew Arnold: *He heard the legions thunder past, And plunged in thought again.* Jeepers, he said (he picked that up from his children), Saint Bypass had something there.

We mustn't be tedious. The tumult and the doubting died; the great Wending Harbor Bridge was finished. It was astoundingly beautiful, as is everything purposely functional: white, fearless, logical and logistical as the proposals of Euclid or the gravities of Newton. The rector even imagined a sermon about it, but wisely he refrained. It would have perplexed his flock, who had had enough woe already. He wanted to remind them that Newton and Euclid obtain only for low velocities. When you get supersonic you have to shift gears to Einstein, Albertus Maximus. The same is so in theology. Christianity doesn't pay off until you attain the speed of Light. The human mind, a filterable virus, is powerfully opaque for the business of slowing down Light.

Now, after noise and misery, the whole human sludge was drained off onto the new highway of escape. The rector pondered his hymnal; the organist (dear old Miss Trefoil), who does the hymns by automatism, never guessed there was a little malice in his choice of number 494 (*Where cross the crowded ways of life, Where sound the cries of race and clan*) and number 541 (*Ten thousand times ten thousand, in sparkling raiment bright*). I even think there was a touch of honest Protestant bile in the second verse of 541 when the rector sang with such brio, *What ringing of a thousand harps.* Frankly, I have no use for any church or creed that doesn't show a tingle of competitive comedy. Heaven is not for pallid saints but raging and risible men.

But now, miracle or mercy, battered and disregarded little Saint Bypass was posed in one of the most perfect vistas of the world, more startling than Saint Peter's in the East (at Oxford) or San Gimignano (in Italy) from which I guess it was imitated.

As you approached, along the now quiet and curly stem of Wending Ways, you saw the humble church through the vast white quadrature of a gigantic concrete frame. Above, patrolled by humorous guards, taxed by small bells of cash, the populace was in flight. The watchmen, like Scotchmen, took their toll and portioned it among Federal, State, and County. These by-passengers didn't know, or care, from what they fled; they imbedded their children in dunnage, and the dogs' ears floated wide out of the window; they were glorious with To and Fro, the Castor and Pollux of Democracy. The Army breathed more freely and turned its five-star mind elsewhere.

Timidly, gratefully, Saint Bypass' own little congregation found its way back to its needed worship. Again they had a lamp to their feet; the way was no longer perverse. And by some chance of acoustic the great bridge that overloomed the church now resonated the deficit clangor of the bells and lifted them to perfect tune.

Abashed and thwarted so long, Saint Bypass-under-the-Bridge found itself famous. An evening paper wrote (rather too lush) about it; even the *New Yorker* handed down one of those vinaigrette and condescending paragraphs. On the great Alba Longa of the overpass, murmurous with rubber and speed, the social dysentery of Vulnerable City rushed by. You could hear, in pauses of the rector's sermon, the hideous hum

(Milton) of people who have to be going somewhere else when we are right here. Ezekiel, who isn't often used as text, came through big in the Concordance: chapter xvii, verse 4, about the young twigs in a land of traffic. And Shakespeare too (thanks to *Bartlett*) was pulpitworthy: "Pass by, and curse thy fill."

A medium-good etcher, on commission, did a plate of the church seen through the accidental perspective of the Bridge. The Chief of Staff, on his way out to see what the atomic bomb laboratory was doing, stopped there to pray. And well he might; well might we all, except the men who write the headlines. Even prayer has to stop somewhere.

So the Lions and the Kiwanis and the vestry were all wrong. Jeepers, Saint Bypass had something after all. The place for saint or scholar to settle is just off the Main Line where everyone is going somewhere else. The faster the stream flows, the more peaceful are its banks. I wouldn't be surprised if Saint Bypass-under-the-Bridge, same as the Air Force, is full strength by Christmas.

An American Gentleman[1]

IT WAS REALLY ODD THAT LAST NIGHT FOR NO DISCOVERABLE reason (except what Keats might have called the ignoble dearth of good narcotics) I picked up Stevenson's *The Dynamiter*. That delicious little prologue in the Cigar Divan, never improved in brio by anyone, is what the bishop was called, social soporific. It sends one off with a smile. But it also sent me off with the familiar thought, why is it never sufficiently suggested that Sherlock Holmes was born out of the ribs of Robert Louis and Fanny Stevenson? Poe and Gaboriau and Dr. Joseph Bell are all very well, but the spark that lit young tinderhearted (*sic*) Conan Doyle was surely the Prince-tobacconist of Bohemia. Even the divan in Rupert Street ("mouse-colored plush") may have fathered the much more famous mouse-colored dressing gown. That was the wicked stinging and punctuating effect of Stevenson's words. They were hypoder-

[1]Copyright, 1947, by Saturday Review Associates, Inc.

mic, needled into one's self. It's amusing to note a recent revival of curiosity in R.L.S. among the stricken middle generation. It is naturally disturbing to the deliterated to find words used with such wasteful delicacy. But the best of him will be forever breathing and forever young, to improve poor Keats's tubercular line. It is a pity that poets have to be outlived to be improved.

I must keep to my theme. Sometime toward the end of '85 or early '86 young Dr. Conan Doyle read *The Dynamiter*. His natural interest in Stevenson (a few years' senior graduate of the same university) was professionally enlarged by the well-known rumor that R.L.S. was a very ill man; an invalid, possibly moribund, at Bournemouth. The famous dedication (in *Underwoods*) to no less than eleven doctors had not then been written (1887, I think?) but there is always a crapevine among medical men, and if Dr. Doyle hadn't been so overdrawn in Southsea he might well have wished to move a few miles Westward to Bournemouth to serve as interne to the immortal Dr. Scott—whose sinister initials were T.B. (Thomas Bodley Scott; see that noble dedication). I think it probable that Dr. Doyle would rather have been Stevenson's medical adviser than anything else he could think of. Young H. G. Wells, then a draper's assistant in Southsea (his employer was a patient of Doyle's), was as ruddy and shrill as only H. G. would have been at nineteen.

The MS of *The Firm of Girdlestone* was already shabby with to-and-fro. The "rustle of the greengrocer's lungs," as Doyle called it, and "the throb of the charwoman's heart" were worth only about eighteen pence a visit. His self-imposed family obligations were large; the hard-earned £250 a year was (as his

Inland Revenue critic wrote on the form) "most unsatisfactory." I imagine him, say some rainywindow evening about Christmas 1885, after a visit to the Southsea Circulatory Library (of which he was the most faithful customer) sitting down to swoon himself with his idol's new book, *More New Arabian Nights: The Dynamiter*. I won't bruise you with all the obvious parallels, but only seven pages in, what did he read:

> "Do you then propose, dear boy, that we should turn detectives?" inquired Challoner.
>
> "Do I propose it? No, sir," cried Somerset. "It is reason, destiny, the plain face of the world, that commands and imposes it. Here all our merits tell; our manners, habit of the world, powers of conversation, vast stores of unconnected knowledge, all that we are and have builds up the character of the complete detective. It is, in short, the only profession for a gentleman."

I could quote more, and zealously apropos; but it will do no one harm to re-examine *The Dynamiter* for himself; the Irgun Zwai Leumi of 1885. The point, sharpened by a hundred razor passages in those preposterous stories (completely witty and completely blah), is that A.C.D. went to bed that night in Bush Villa with a new idea in his simple and workable occiput.

It was not only a detective that he had in occiput, but even, God forgive him, a Mormon interlude. He had no idea, nor does it matter, that he was unconsciously mismating Edgar Poe's detective with Fanny Stevenson's appalling Mormon feuilleton. But if you want to suffer, which is part of a literary critic's duty, reread *A Study in Scarlet* (written 1886) and then that grievous chapter in *The Dynamiter*, "The Story of the Destroying Angel." He did it again, thirty-five years later, in *The Valley of Fear*. He never shook off the unconscious influence of that emphatic woman; nor did anyone else.

The intimations of literary heredity, the cross-fertilities of suggestion, are more subtle than any bookish Burbank has ever put in *précis*. No one has ever had the courage, let us say, to suggest the bloodstream osmosis between Hemingway and Kipling (of which, prudentially, Hemingway is least aware). But the exciting thing, in the woe and wizardry of art (I beg you remember this), is that one man's poison can be another man's meat. The most forgettable thing one artist ever did (Stevenson's futile, delightful *Dynamiter*, for instance) can be the accidental takeoff and jet-bomb for another man's felicity. Neither of them will know it. Only the true lover of human frequencies and modulations will ever guess; and will keep it to himself.

I said it was odd; this was what I meant. I fell on sleep thinking about Doyle's subconscious impulse from Stevenson. I thought about it again, as one does, this morning, brooding in the only privacy that still exists, the bathtub. (Much more private than Mr. Hoover's two aspiring secrecies; prayer and fishing.) It was in my mind, and futile at that, to remark Doyle's unconscious increment from R.L.S. That leads one to think (few people do?) of their own impulsives from behind the swing. I thought of Don Marquis, and Simeon Strunsky, and William Hazlitt, from whom I myself have been ungrateful and unconscious to plunder. It is the people from whom you steal who are the zodiac over your Grand Central. People who are just catching trains don't have time to look at the ceiling.

I said it was odd: about midmorning I went down to the depot, got my copy of the New York *Times*, and saw that our dear old Lloyd Osbourne died yesterday. *Loia*, as the Samoans called him, unspoiled old innocent, was perhaps the greatest

American Boy (barefoot, with cheek) since Whittier and Mark Twain. Who remembers the immortal dedication:

> To LLOYD OSBOURNE
> An American Gentleman
> In accordance with whose classic
> taste the following narrative has been
> designed. . . .

Just about fifty years ago I had an earache; in the therapy of that era, I was put to bed with a baked onion poulticed on me, and given a paper-bound piracy to read. How well I remember it, as soon as I got interested in the Admiral Benbow I forgot my ear, and haven't thought of it since. But I never forgot (I always read all the front-matter of books; sometimes it's the best of them) L. O., the American Gentleman. Nor do I forget that he was collaborator in what shrewd judges (for instance Rudyard Kipling) have said is a Test Book. *The Wrong Box* (1889) is the kind of book you don't mention except to Initiates (as Kipling said). I have always felt a little bashful about it because my father read it on his honeymoon. It was then, and remains for those who know a smile from a smirk, "judicious levity." Twenty-five years ago I used to see Lloyd Osbourne around the mid-forties, perhaps at the Coffee House Club. I never told him, and I'm sorry, that when driving the highways of North America I often thought of him. They have a way of painting, before arterial crossings, the sedative abbreviation SLO. Always, putting on the brakes, I used to think of him. His full name was Samuel Lloyd Osbourne—the last of a relentful generation. He entertained angels awares.

Never make up your mind (if that's what it is) about literature until you have no personal interest in it. All I'm trying to say is that just as Lloyd Osbourne's rainy day in Scotland in 1881 helped to create *Treasure Island*, so did his stepfather's illness in Bournemouth in 1884–85 help to beget Sherlock Holmes.

Piety is the love of things that have been loved before, by better men than yourself. There is no piety if you don't say it.

Another Letter
to Lord Chesterfield[1]

February 7, 1945

LONG YEARS HAVE PAST, MY LORD, SINCE I WAS FIRST APPE-
tized and then feduced by the publick ingratiations of your
merchandize. You know from Mr. BOSWELL that I had always
a high opinion of the fedative influence of fmoking, though
not then a participant. But your repetitive folicitations invited
experiment, and I formed a guft for tobacco. To enjoyment
fupervened habit; habit hardened to immoderation; immoderation became neceffity. What had been rare and cafual grew
conftant and compulfive.

And now, my Lord, when bound in aromatic chains and firmly
habituated to your foothing benifons, they are coldly with-
drawn. I wait a ftranger in your outward rooms, or am repulfed
from your counter. Daily I peregrinate a whole fynod of tobac-
conifts; vain vifitation without a word of encouragement. It is
but the triumph of hope over experience. Yet alfo daily,

whether in publick print and billboard or in the garrulities of aether, I am advertized to profecute my indulgence.

Is a Merchant, my Lord, one who aggravates abftinence by reminders of loft luxury? Who looks with frigid unconcern upon a man famifhed for a fag, yet exafperates deprivation with renewed enticements and coloured placards?

A denicotined fociety may be numbered among the viciffitudes of Compleat War. But chearful confuetude is not lightly ruptured. A chafm is made which nothing can fill up. The world's ftock of harmlefs pleafure is diminifhed. If all the tobaccos were fent to our military abroad, no citizen but would acquiefce in equal forbearance; but even the foldiers defiderate, and write home begging auxiliary fupply.

The honeft tradesman is impelled to embarraffed favouritifm. He muft juggle his petty ftock among cuftomers beft known or moft roughly infiftent. He is cajoled without fincerity and reproached without caufe. In epidemick anxiety the populace vibrate from fhop to fhop, or elongate endurance at ftreet corners to feize trafh goods unknown before. *Nil fumabilis a me alienum puto!* Who is pleafed to abftain from what more flexile confcience can procure? Fair market is blackened by fubterfuge and turpitude. Let all be abftinent, or none. Would fcarcity be abated by one Smokelefs Day a week? If fo, let it be œcumenical, from White Houfe to Grub Street.

To continue publick fuggeftion where there is no profpect of private relief is either wanton fport or ftark infenfibility. I fpeak not in mere felf-love, for months ago, in apprehenfion of paucity, I fecreted in fafe-depofit at Corn-Exchange a packet of your Lordfhip's wares, for ignition on the Laft Day.

Dies iræ, dies illa,
folvet fæclum in favilla;

your claſſics, my Lord, were formerly competent. But, as I wrote you 190 years ago, your favours have been delayed till I am indifferent and ſmoke anything; till I am churliſh and cannot offer them; till I have learned the uſe of a pipe and do not need them. I warned you: it is ill to trifle with the humours of a lexicographer.

Give me for the future, my Lord, either flattering hope or candid knowledge; or a balanced blend of both; and let us keep our friendſhip in repair. So I may be

Your Lordſhip's moſt humble
moſt craving servant
SAM. JOHNSON
(*per Chriſtopher Morley*)

A *Christmas Story*
without Slush[1]

SURELY ONE OF THE MOST UNUSUAL THINGS IN THE WORLD: a Christmas Story without slush. It makes me sad to think that the one perfect reader for it, the man who more than any other would have delighted in its economy and skill, never saw it. I mean, of course, Charles Dickens. How much Dickens might have learned from it, if he had been capable of learning! I am quite serious when I say that, as a story, *The Blue Carbuncle* is a far better work of art than the immortal *Christmas Carol*. The latter, canonized by over a hundred years of sentiment, is more legendary than legible. It contains deathless scenes of sheer genius, but all clanked and labored together by a heavy drag of mechanical framework. And, as a collector, I would rather have Sidney Paget's original drawings for this story, in the old *Strand*

[1]Written as preface for the Baker Street Irregulars' edition of *The Blue Carbuncle*, by A. Conan Doyle, still available from their sales manager, Mr. Louis Greenfield, 51 East 10 St., New York 3, N.Y. Copyright, 1948, by The Baker Street Irregulars, Inc.

Magazine for January 1892, than Leech's color plates for the *Carol*.

How long does it take for any piece of writing to become a classic? There are still fine old people, in their 70's and 80's, who must remember reading *The Blue Carbuncle* in that old magazine with its pale blue cover picturing Southampton Street, Strand; or in the Harper edition of the *Adventures of Sherlock Holmes*, autumn 1892. Harper tried as nearly as possible to imitate, in cloth binding, the blue tint of the magazine. Readers thought of it, naturally, as just another adventure of Sherlock Holmes. It never fell into the Trade's most profitable groove as a "Christmas story." It was a just-after-Christmas story, and it was good entertainment. They didn't (and mostly readers shouldn't) realize it was superb art. It hasn't a word too many or too few, and it doesn't rely (like O. Henry's famous *Gift of the Magi*) on sleight of hand. It nowhere breaks its chosen mood.

It's interesting, by the way, to reflect that both Dickens and Doyle were about the same age (say 31 or 32) when *Carol* and *Carbuncle* were written. It's a critical age, when hope and disgust and domestic overheads are all in unstable balance. The frustrated young doctor who wrote *The Blue Carbuncle* probably had no idea it was a masterpiece in its kind. But a great many devotees quite independently have learned to reread it during the Christmas octave. I used to wish that Franklin Roosevelt would sometimes vary his (widely publicized) habit of reading the *Carol* aloud to his family on Christmas Eve. After all, he was also a Baker Street Irregular, and (if I know anything about families) the younger generation would have enjoyed the change. But if you pause to think, there were strong psychological reasons for F.D.R.'s fixation on Dickens. Tiny Tim also

had a leg brace; and I feel sure that F.D.R. got an annual guffaw
out of Dickens's malicious allusion to the U.S.A. Even in his
little homily of love, Dickens, like Jack Priestley, couldn't resist
a barb for the gigantic daughter of the West. Scrooge, you will
remember, found some of his fiscal paper as worthless as "a mere
United States security."

But let us stick to our goose. Here is a post-Christmas story
for frostbitten people. It happened on Friday, December 27,
1889. Dr. Watson, not very long married, had quite properly
spent Christmas and Boxing Day with his wife and patients.
Then Mrs. Watson went to visit her aunt, of whom we know
too little.[2] The Doctor, though too mannerly to boast of it, had
an evening or so off leash. There is no other genteel way to
account for his double visits to Baker Street on December 27.
He called on Holmes to wish him, in his restrained way, "the
compliments of the season." That is the first frosty phrase to
remember. Not a Merry Old Christmas, not Jocund Yule; just
the bashful British meiosis, Compliments of the Season. Wary
old Watson, one of Britain's great understatesmen. No emotional Heilige Nacht, no Tannenbaum, no vast substantial
Fezziwigs, no lachrymous Yuletide yowling. Compliments of
the Season, Old Boy; and how are you, Holmes?

We know how he was. Particularly if we have relished Sidney Paget's drawings (*Strand*, January 1892) we have memorized those tantalizing glimpes into the immortal sitting-room:
the horsehair sofa, the dressing gown, the pipe-rack. What
pipes! How Dunhill would be shocked: a few dirty clays and
straight-stem bulldogs, and the cherrywood for disputation.

[2] I believe she was actually Mrs. Cecil Forrester, of Camberwell, where
Mrs. Watson had been employed as governess. The family grew so fond
of Mary Morstan, later Mrs. Watson, that she called Mrs. Forrester
"Aunt."

Never a droopy bowl as the movies and California vintners insist, their horrible curly calabashes and processed chin-briars. After Holmes had his tooth knocked out in Charing Cross Station (see *The Adventure of the Empty House*) he had to wear falsettoes. He couldn't denture a gooseneck pipe.

But more minutiae. The basket chair. Few Americans know what is a basket chair ("Minty's Varsity Chair") invented (at Oxford?) to help students fall asleep beside the fireplace. Look closer still into Paget's drawings: see Watson's velvet-collared topcoat, and Ascot tie. See Holmes's caped ulster; very dear to me, because my dear Old Man (my father), when he emigrated to U.S.A. in 1887, had just such a garment. It was pale sandy-color with reticulations of green. He wore it until about 1900, when we moved to Baltimore; then my Mother cut it down to be a dressing gown for me. I wore it to and from the bathroom until about 1910. Then my younger brothers took over. It was very likely re-dyed, like Holmes's own, which experts remember started purple, then mouse, and then grey. The gradual solstitial fading of Holmes's dressing gown is one of the statutory documentations of life as it happens. It is one of the accidentals that prove that Doyle was a great unconscious artist, as all artists are.

This wonderful wintry story of the Blue Carbuncle offers all sorts of opportunities to scholars. It has everything that a Xmas fable wants: frost-crystals on the windows, brisk outdoor walking, and Holmes's slippers warming by the fire. It has in it one of the most famous passages in fiction, the deductions made from the old battered and greasy derby hat. That is plainly an attempt to imitate the equally famous series of inferences made from H. Watson's gold watch in *The Sign of the Four;* and even excelled some years later by the glorious deductions made from *Whitaker's Almanac* (the predecessor of Golenpaul-Kieran's) in *The Valley of Fear*. That is what fiction exists for, to make delightful the impossible and unbelieved.

Are we scholars? Are we talking about the Impossible? How could our hero Sherlock get advertisements into all the afternoon papers by mid-morning? How come the plumber was working on Sunday at the Cosmopolitan Hotel? (If Friday was the 27th, the 22nd was Sunday.) How come that Sherlock's fire "crackled"? It was certainly a soft-coal fire, which never crackles? Why does Sherlock say that the solution was "its own reward"? We know perfectly well that he must have taken a percentage of the Countess of Morcar's offer (£1000) because he had these items at least to pay: the cost of advertisements in seven or more evening papers; the sovereign bet at Covent Garden; the cost of the four-wheeler, and the fresh goose, and the broken window. I am perfectly sure that on the morning of Saturday, December 28th, Holmes (still feeling the holiday spirit) went round to the shop on Tottenham Court Road, paid for the broken window, and charged it to account. The Xmas goose, judging by Breckinridge's mark-up, cost Holmes (per Mrs. Hudson) probably 16/6, and I dare say he wrote off the woodcock too as "Entertaining client." Much has been said about Holmes's housekeeping, but no one has remarked his passion for meat, and bird-game. We have records of his meals of grouse, pheasant, partridge, woodcock, and pâté de foie gras; cold beef, and eggs, and oysters. But he never ate fish; he can't have been English? There was some talk about trout in the Shoscombe case, but only as pretext.

Scholars, I said? What was poor Henry Baker doing in the British Museum? You may or may not notice that when he comes to Baker Street (I wish we knew which newspaper it was where he saw the advt.? Myself I think it was *The Star*) he quotes Horace (*Satires*, I. iv, 62). Actually he misquotes, *disjecta membra*. So I think he was doing research, reading and devilling and misquoting, for Dr. Thorneycroft Huxtable's *Sidelights on Horace*, which had a European vogue. Dr. Huxtable was too busy, as schoolmaster (see *The Adventure of the Priory School*), to do his collations for himself. I know the place, here called The Alpha, where Henry Baker joined the goose-club. It is at the corner of Museum and Great Russell Streets. It used to have, in the old days (about 1924), the most beautiful crosscut rose-and-white jambon of ham waiting for slice behind the bar. And crisp crusty secants of fresh bread.

Ham makes me think of *The Pink 'Un*, that Breckinridge had in his coat pocket. How many of our young readers will know, and how do people know if you don't tell them, *The Pink 'Un* is a sporting paper, printed on pink sheets, something like our American *Police Gazette?*

There are many kinds of readers; the best and brightest of them probably wish to be amused, not to deduce nor infer. For either kind this chilblain comedy is perfect. It is as traditional as Homer, as corny-modern as Billy Rose, the suitor of O. Henry. You can read into it subtleties the author had no notion of, for instance that the crook Ryder and his girl-friend Kitty Cusack got the simple plumber to the hotel on Sunday (December 22) because that would be the day when the Countess of Morcar was out at a party. Or you can worry about what is a *commissionaire*, one of the corps of uniformed veterans (G.I.'s) founded in 1859, who run errands and take messages and do doorman work at hotels and theatres. So read the story first (aloud, if you have any friends patient enough) and don't worry about details.

Years ago I amused myself one Xmas by making a model stage-set for a toy theatre, to represent this story on Baker Street. I fixed cellophane windows crystallized with frost; the coal fire, the scuttle, the fiddle, and Holmes's slippers. There was the fresh goose (16 shillings and 6d) on the sideboard, and of course the decanter of brandy, Watson's universal specific. The detective, in purple gown, lounged among his crumpled papers, and studied the old billycock with forceps and lens. Watson was just coming in at the door, carrying (what Sidney Paget forgot) his medical bag. My truly great invention was the Sherlock Holmes Cherubs that hovered in air looking in the window. They were the face of the Great Sleuth, in accipitrine and oblique perspective, but supported by feathery wings. It seemed to me a wonderful Idea, uniting both motives: the dominant skull of Sherlock (whose hair was receding fast on top, according to Sidney Paget) and the sacred wings of the Season. Some of them had little deerstalker hats for the wintry weather. I wish I could find my drawing for that scene. I couldn't ever do it again; no artist can do anything twice. But I hope to persuade some young sculptor to design a Sherlock Holmes Cherub as a Xmas Card for the Baker Street Irregulars.

This most kindly and unintentional of Christmas Stories belongs in what that good man Oscar Firkins (of the University of Minnesota) once called "the warm little hollow between Christmas and New Year." That should be, if human beings were as sensitive as one would like to suppose, a moment of peace.

Bronzino's Mixture[1]

IT WAS DOVE DULCET, THE LITERARY AGENT. HE DOESN'T usually travel on my branch of the railroad, and I thought he looked a little glassy-eyed; but I couldn't let so old a friend escape without greeting, and sat down beside him. After we got out of the noise of the tunnel he began to talk.

"Yes," he said, "I'm often reproached for not having what it would be luxurious not to have."

"But you, of course, have it," I suggested. "What on earth can it be?"

"My life is so embarrassing," he moaned (he's rather like Reggie Fortune sometimes), "because when I'm truly intent on my private fancies I forget civilized convenance. I'm almost afraid of meeting an old pal, or someone who made a shortcut into being an old pal, for fear I won't identify him."

"My name is Chris Morley," I said. "As a matter of fact I'm

[1]Copyright, 1947, by Saturday Review Associates, Inc.

one of your quite profitable clients. You've made my life embarrassing too. Sometimes you sold my stuff before I'd even
written it. Then I *had* to do it, and everyone was disappointed.
Nothing spoils a story like writing it."

It only takes a little sharp dialogue to brighten Dove up, and
he brightened.

"I can tell you before we get to Jamaica," he said. "I'll have
to change there and go back to Woodside. I can see, by the
fact you're here, that I'm on the wrong train."

I supposed Dove had been celebrating; but this is what he
told me:

What I have is memory. Not social or factual or quiz-pro-
gram memory, but something damnably different: esthetic
memory, total emotional recall. Suppose I want to reread something I enjoyed before. I need probably three years before I
can do so. I don't forget fast enough. That's the tragedy of the
book business. All other appetites renew themselves quickly.

In my profession I have to read new stuff all the time, in type-
script or in galley proof. I have to make up my mind what I
think about it, and what others will think. But secretly, old
client, I don't much care. I made up my mind long ago what
sort of stuff I enjoy.

Page Freud, Jung, Adler, Horney? Why, sure! Retreat from
reality? Exactly so! When we mature and murify, when the
Iceman Cometh (Saint Frigid!), we retire like Walt Whitman,
to the certainties suitable to us.

You know that midtown street where there face each other
a famous bookstore and a notable bivalve-monger? I frequent
them both, because they are efficient and not arty. Bibliophiles
from one side and bon mangeurs from the other meet and ex-

change curiosities. Finnan haddie or pigs-in-blankets (though more costly) can be matched against Penguin Books or Oxford Classics. While Gus the waiter is on safari for devilled bones, or Harry the bar is at the other end of the counter, you may think of a book your friend ought to read. There'll be plenty of time to hare across and buy it at Bronzino's before Gus is back from that overworked kitchen. You might even be able to detax it as Entertaining the Trade. That's how they learn about Literature.

So one day my friend and I, preceding our finnan haddie with a little gin-and-ginger, talked about books we wished we could read again. Was it Conrad? Conan Doyle? Cutcliffe Hyne? Frank Stockton? Even Anthony Hope, or Rider Haggard, or O. Henry? I know it was some corn du siècle. At their nadir (and how often they were) they were terrible. Actually I think we were talking of George Gissing, his sensitive sad short stories, rarely noticed by anyone. Do you know how much better they are than his laborious novels? Nor did he. But we had read them, my friend and I, when they and we were young. Whatever you call it (scrapple or haggis or umbles or toad-in-the-hole), everyone needs his own kind of tripe. As we used to say, in the old newspaper days (but never in print), Don't muzzle the Ochs that treadeth the corn. Nothing is so dangerous, in print, as a quotation from the Bible.

My friend had never read *Ryecroft* (the most warmblooded of all books-about-books), so again I questioned Gus. He said, "Did you say gin an' haddie or finnan haddie?" and resumed his bustling trot. I flitted across to Bronzino's Bookstore. I wanted to consult Lorry Lorrequer, who has charge of Editions. Bless his heart, he is almost the only man who was raised on the very same hooey that I was. As we said simultaneously one time, after several snorts, we are hooey generis. From Gus's service tray I snatched a roll in the likelihood that Lorry wouldn't have had his lunch. He hadn't; he was being demure on the telephone, in the act of vending some Collector. (They always call at lunch time. They themselves have ulcers and can't eat.) I waited, mannerly. Then he tilted an ear, and I mumbled, "Come over to Billy Bivalve and have a Ryecroft and soda."

"Not likely," he whispered. "I'm on the beam, selling Complete Millay in a binding. We always keep her in Morocco, or the Levant, just on the chance."

"It's certainly safer," I said. "But it ties up a lot of capital? I hope those de luxe binders give plenty of time?"

Lorry looked pained; like what they call in catalogues *bruised, slightly shaken*. Patiently but firmly he finished his telephone conversation, writing down something on an order slip. I could see it was in the bag—indeed I could almost hear the levantine binder dropping the bag.

"If you haven't got *Ryecroft*," I said, "how about *The House of Cobwebs?* Remember? Constable, 1906. My friend hasn't read that. Gosh, how I envy him! Those dim, desiccated, despondent stories! Their lurking, lugubrious laughter!"

His face grew bleak. "You know perfectly well it's out of print. I'd lend your friend my own copy, but I read it in bed last week, and I'm going to do it again tonight. It's the only thing that gets me through the Wedding-Present Season; all half morocco and half literature."

"But how can you, so soon?" I cried. "Oh, Man of Feeling, remember the reading we first knew, when we were lifted to glory and learned the nobility of print? How rekindle that dazzle of innocence? The thrill of our boyhood, when Kaa and Baloo and Bagheera broke the bandar-log at the Cold Lairs? When the *Narcissus* went over on her beam ends and the chapel-crazed lunatic fights his way back to the galley: 'As long as she swims I will cook!' Or damn it all, poetry too—*The Eve of St. Agnes,* or Ulysses on the beach with Calypso. No, I guess I didn't really twig that then. Very few of the teachers do, even now."

It was hard to understand him for a minute or so; he was busily chewing the roll I brought. It sounded something like this:

"Surely you know that if everyone were like us there wouldn't be any book trade at all? I beg you, don't encourage people to feel that writing can be so important."

While he surmounted a crusty knob I was able to say, "Damme, writing isn't just showing-off; it's showing-in."

He liked that, and tried to show me so by an affectionate grin that showered out a whole fringe of crumbs.

"I want to read *Ryecroft* again," I said, "and *Mycroft,* and *Pyecroft,* and even *Beecroft.* But I can't. I've read them all within a year, and I haven't forgotten enough. Keats, my goodness, Keats! Empty some dull opiate to the drains! You know, when I was a teacher one time I had a class of boys in Keats, one of them pulled on me the accidental atom bomb of genius. He thought Keats's Morphean amulet was a Morphine Omelet. Listen, Lorry, close the magic casements so we can open them again!"

It was his mouth he opened; I could see the last of the baker's chaw disappearing, but just then his secretary said, "Atwater on the wire again, Mr. Lorrequer. He wants to know, haven't you got Millay in Full Vellum?"

He was really annoyed. After deglutition he said, "Tell him the only Full Vellum we have is Robert W. Service." And he added the most intelligent thing ever said about print since Gutenberg, who said, "If I like it I'll print it, whether they pay their bills or not." But what Lorry said was: "Why would you expect people to be any smarter about their reading than they are about love, or politics, religion, or peepshows?"

He leaned over to a cupboard behind his desk; I had always thought it probably contained unbound prints of Felicien Rops, the early Clara Tice, and those Japanese esoterica that neither MacArthur nor Hirohito ever saw. These are the Edition Man's last line of offense after a heavy customer has forced him to lunch.

No, it was something quite different. I saw a row of little phials with a pale dusky-pearly paregoric-looking liquor. He took one out and shook it; it clouded like a Baker Street fog. "Here you are," he said. "Medicine for case like yours, as Walt Whitman said. We invented it for the reprint trade."

There was a small label on the bottle: BRONZINO'S MIX-TURE. *Lethamins G and D. Caution, take only as directed.*

"The true Lethean liqueur," said Lorry. "This really wipes your eye. Take a small slug after finishing a book, you forget it at once and can read it again like fresh—if you want to. The greater impression the book made on you the better you forget. Washes your mind."

"And the reviews of the book, and the ads—do you forget them too?" I asked hopefully.

Lorry smiled. How well Collectors know that sad, faint, alluring, and detachable smile.

"I always keep a bottle in the medicine cabinet," he said. "When I read in the middle of the night I dose myself and go off like a movie star. Just remember, **you have to** finish the book before using the mixture."

"Mr. Lorrequer," said his young woman, "Atwater's on the wire again. Wants to know is Irwin Edman in a binding yet?"

"We have Edman gilt top, but only in fabrikoid."

"He says," she reported, "if you haven't got Edman, Santa-yana might do?"

Lorry, even Lorry, was getting a little impatient. "Tell him we have Dr. Johnson's *Lives of the Poets,* first edition, four volumes in full calf, only $40. By the time he's read that, Edman will be in rag, and probably in a box."

People were pressing forward to ask how you could get your name put on the waiting list to join the Book-of-the-Month Club, so I grabbed a bottle of his literary laudanum and fled to the counter near the door where they keep reprints of Conrad: *Typhoon,* and *The Nigger,* and that other one (I never mention its title; the perfect fancy of man overtaken by Fate; few will ever read or ponder it; I have small assurance of man's curiosity for poetic truth.) But before I went back into Bivalve's, to see if Gus had yet brought the finnan haddie, I took a quick taste of Bronzino's Mixture.

It went down like smooth-sliding Mincius: sweetly tart, and fumy, and ticklish on the tongue. I stood there on the pavement, mouthing it over, and thought wouldn't it be wonderful! To take it as chaser after reading anything, and so forget the story at once. I know now why poor De Quincey drank tincture of opium. The enemies of art are those who remember too well, and who carry into it their own prejudicial private circumstances. That's being a customer, not a collaborator. I don't give a damn for reading unless I can create it along with the struggling fool who wrote it.

But it only applies, Lorry warned me, to the last thing you have read. You must be sure to know what you want to forget. That's not always easy. There are lots of things that memory can turn sweet.

So if I was kind of dopey (Dove concluded; gathering his hat and coat and bag; we were just coming in to the smooth-sliding platform at Jamaica, L. I.) it's because I took a slug of Bronzino's Mixture this afternoon. The amazing thing is, it works.

There was only a moment, but when I really need to know I can ask questions fast.

"Wait a minute," I cried. "What was it you were so keen to forget? Was it the Long Island timetable? Or don't you even remember what it was you've forgotten?"

"Good old boy," he said kindly, with a peculiar smile. "It was something of yours."

Codeine (7 Per Cent)[1]

I HADN'T SEEN DOVE DULCET, FORMER LITERARY AGENT AND amateur detective, for a long time—not since he went into Naval Intelligence in '39. But last winter the Baker Street Irregulars, that famous club of Sherlock Holmes devotees, invited him to be a guest at their annual dinner. Dulcet is shy and would have preferred not to speak, but of course he was called on and made a very agreeable little impromptu which I supposed the B & O from Washington had given him time to think out.

What Dulcet did was propose a toast to Sherlock Holmes's unknown sister. She was a good deal younger than either Mycroft or Sherlock, he suggested. The basis of his fancy was Sherlock's famous remark to Miss Hunter when she was offered that dubious position as governess at the Copper Beeches. "It is not the situation which I should like to see a sister of mine

[1]Copyright, 1945, by The American Mercury, Inc.

apply for," said Sherlock Holmes. Dulcet maintained that no man would say that unless he actually *did* have a sister; and offered ingenious suggestions why Watson had never mentioned her.

The Irregulars, who were getting a bit noisy by then (it was late in the evening), accused Dulcet of being "whimsical," and chaffed him a good deal. There's something in Dove's innocent demeanor, his broad bland face and selvage of saffron-colored hair under an ivory scalp, that encourages good-natured teasing. He was twitted about the supposed inefficiency of our Intelligence Services—how G2, for instance, was caught actually moving its offices on D-Day, with all its phones and devices cut off so they didn't even know what was happening. He replied that maybe that was exactly what G2 wanted people to think; perhaps they had Planned It That Way. He suggested gently (he speaks in a voice so soft that people really keep quiet in order to listen) that sometimes the Intelligence people work longer ahead than we suppose. I noticed that he paused then a moment, as though he had more to say and thought better of it. "And now, gentlemen," he concluded, "you'll pardon me if I excuse myself and retire. I've got one of those delicious fin de siècle rooms here at the old Murray Hill and I can't wait to get to it. You know the kind of thing, a big brass bedstead, and lace drapes, and a rose-colored secretary with wonderful scrollwork." Of course this gave the stags a laugh, and I caught a small private wink from him as he sat down. So presently I followed him up to his room.

"That was an ingenious surmise of yours," I said, "about Holmes having a sister."

"No surmise at all," he said. "I knew her. Or rather, to be exact, I know her daughter. Violet Hargreave; she works for me."

"Good heavens!" I exclaimed. "*Hargreave?* The New York Police Department? As mentioned in the *Dancing Men?*"

"Of course. Violet's mother married Sherlock's friend, Wilson Hargreave. She was Sibyl Holmes, one of the Holmeses who stayed in this country. I didn't want to mention names at your dinner. In our kind of job you don't do it. When I went into Intelligence I took Violet with me. She's absolutely indispensable. Wonderful gift for languages; we use her mostly as an agent overseas."

If I had asked further questions Dove would have shut up; he always says that the first shot you take in Government work is a transfusion of clam-juice. But we are very old friends and he trusts me. He poured me a drink and then fetched his wallet from under his pillow.

"I had this in my pocket tonight," he said, taking out a letter. "I would have loved to mention it when one of your members was talking about cryptography, codes, ciphers, and so on. The best codes are the simplest, not methodical at all but based on some completely personal association. She's safe at home now, so I can show you how Violet used to get her stuff out of Berlin when it wasn't easy. Sometimes it was only a few words on a picture postcard; the Nazis never seemed to suspect anything so naïve as that. When she had more to say she used some stationery she swiped from the Museum of Natural History, to look professional, and then overprinted a new letterhead."

I examined the paper. At the top of the sheet was the legend AMERICAN MUSEUM OF NATURAL HISTORY, and under it:

Professor Challenger's Expedition
Oceanic Ornithology
c/o S.Y. Matilda Briggs

"She couldn't get much on a postcard, not with a handwriting like that," I said, glancing at the lines of large heavily-inked script. "Very different from the small neat hand of her uncle."

"She has several handwritings, as occasion requires. Go ahead and read the letter."

It went thus:

> Dear Friend:
>
> Everything very interesting, and German scientists most helpful. Hope to come back by way of Pacific, Hawaii and Alleutians, studying migrations of gulls and goonies. If can take Kodiak will have wonderful pictures. Goonies (*phalacrocorax carbo*, a kind of cormorant, dangerous to lighthouse keepers) have regular schedule, fly Midway or Wake in October, Alleutians in June. Hope to get mail at Honolulu before you take up Conk-Singleton papers.
>
> Yours always,
VIOLET H. HARGREAVE

"She really is an ornithologist, isn't she," I said.

"So the Berlin censor thought, as he let it come through. Does nothing else strike you?"

"Well, I haven't got my convex lens," I said. "Are there any secret watermarks in the paper? The only thing I notice is that surely a scientific investigator should spell geography correctly. Isn't there only one l in Aleutians?"

"Good man. Of course that would tickle the German censor; he'd just think another ignorant American. You can be quite sure any member of the Holmes family would know how to spell. That's our private signal. Whenever Violet spells something wrong I know there's a double meaning. So the gulls and goonies are Japs."

"Say, she's good! And the allusions to the Holmes cases—

sure, I get it. Cormorant and lighthouse keeper—that suggests politician; the story of the *Veiled Lodger;* it means get this warning across to the government. But what about Conk-Singleton?"

"Don't you remember the end of the *Six Napoleons?* Holmes says, before you get out the Conk-Singleton papers *put the pearl in the safe.* Just what we didn't do with Pearl Harbor."

"But what's the date of this letter?" I exclaimed. "Why, its spring of '41, six months before Pearl Harbor."

"I told you we have to work ahead of time," Dove said. "Violet had just been tipped off, in Berlin, about the secret terms of the German-Japanese alliance. Hitler told the Japs he'd be in Moscow by Christmas, they'd be perfectly safe to strike in December. And you can check those goony dates, which by the way are correct for the bird migrations. The Japs landed at Attu and Kiska in June, just as she said."

"I always wondered what they thought they could do up there on those godforsaken rocks."

"Maybe they were attracted by the name of that group. Ever notice it on the map? The Rat Islands."

I was beginning to get the inwardness of this Baker Street code. "Goodness, even the name of the yacht, *Matilda Briggs*—in the *Sussex Vampire;* why, yes, that was the story of the Giant Rat of Sumatra——"

"For which the world *is not prepared,*" Dove finished for me.

"Golly, the State Department must have turned handsprings when you decoded this for them."

Dove was discreetly silent.

I looked over the letter once more. "Kodiak . . . they

thought she meant Kodak. I suppose you couldn't make any mistake, it was sure to refer to the Japanese?"

"Well, there Violet was really cute. You spoke of the handwriting."

"Yes, she must have used a very broad pen, a stub."

"She picked up the idea from her Uncle Mycroft. Don't you remember his immortal remark, in *The Greek Interpreter*—about the letter written with a J-pen, that is a stub pen—by a middle-aged man with a weak constitution."

"I guess that's me," I said feebly. "Still I don't get it."

"J-pen, Japan."

We finished what Dove called our auld lang snort. I was thinking hard. "Whenever you get a letter with a wrong spelling," I said guiltily, "do you suspect a secret meaning?—Gosh, do you suppose when broadcasters mispronounce a word on the radio it's really a code?"

"Get out of here," said Dove. "I want my rest."

Hitch Your Wagon—[1]

I HAD BEEN MOST OF THE DAY AT THE STATE DEPARTMENT, and you know how tiresome that is. (It was Dove Dulcet talking, the literary detective.) I had to wait a long time for my appointments, and had plenty of leisure to study the Great Seal of the United States which is so generously displayed. I had no lunch, and when I got aboard the Congressional at 4 P.M. I felt I had earned a drink.

Evidently many others had the same idea; when I got to what the railroad timetables call a buffet lounge (you do the lounging, the P.R.R. does the buffeting) there was only one empty seat. It was at a table with three men who were feeling no pain. I was in a mood of solitude and not eager to sit with what my genteel friend the deputy-acting-under-assistant secretary calls knackers. They were far from State Department in demeanor; shedding cigarette ashes all over the starched tablecloth; if they ever wore striped pants they were underpants. Still there was a kind of genial dynamism about them that was rather refreshing, after a day of so much shoe-polish. I took the seat.

I was brooding what to have when the waiter came reeling down the aisle with a large tray. He addressed the three talkers: "Yessuh, yessuh, just what you ordered; thirteen Martinis." He deftly set them down in a cluster without spilling much. As you know, I'm literal; I couldn't help counting them. Thirteen Martinis, each with an olive of large displacement. Then he waited for my command.

Before I could speak the man next me said, "I beg your pardon, sir, would you take our extra Martini? We had to order thirteen for luck, but that leaves one over. If you would accept it you'd be doing us a favor. Just let me spoon out the olive. We have to eat those, it's protocol."

It was rather like the beginning of R. L. Stevenson's *New Arabian Nights*. I hoped, as did Prince Florizel in the story, that the spirit was not one of mockery. But the strangers were so cheerful in manner I felt it would be boorish to refuse. I took the goblet, bowed to them, and drank. Each of the others instead of drinking picked up an olive and bowed as he nibbled it. They made no attempt to force me into palaver and I retired to my usual train-reading, an attempt to discover what those topical weeklies mean by reporting the news "in three dimensions." But I couldn't help noticing that my companions didn't drink their cocktails, only dipped out the fruit. Could they be travelling inspectors from some Martini factory? Looking for what Shakespeare called "olives of endless age"? (By which he meant Lasting Peace.)

By the time we got to Baltimore the drinks, except mine, had mostly slopped over onto the cloth. The three genials kept saluting each other; each time they ate an olive they said *Aloha nui nui*. By some of their remarks about *wahinis* and *hoomali-mali* I guessed they were old service men from the Pacific. Or maybe numerologists, for they seemed to have a fixation on arithmetic. One of them counted the Martini goblets with his finger and said, "That leaves 36 to come."

I was feeling more friendly by then, and spoke up. "I can't buy 36," I said, "but I'd be happy to offer you gentlemen a round, if you'll really drink it."

They were most polite. "We're very sorry, sir," they said, "we'd like to join you but this is a matter of ritual. It's on expense account. Our next has to be brandy, and we really drink it. The Martinis were just to get exactly 13 olives."

"I'll order a highball and stand by," I said. "You may need help getting off the train."

They told the puzzled waiter to clear away the unconsumed Martinis. "Bring us 12 brandies," they said. Then they summoned the steward and insisted on a big balloon-glass. Into this they poured the individual servings and used it as a loving cup. They beamed gaily at me as they swigged in turn. "This is 3-star," they said. "Twelve 3-stars makes 36."

They were getting merry; but by the time we crossed the Susquehanna they had a little difficulty in saying it.

"You see how it works out," said one. "13 olives plus 36 cognac make 49." I knew he was an old Army man because he called it *cone*-yack.

"God Bless America!" exclaimed another. "I won't say more because it's copyrighted."

" 'Where the air is full of sunlight and the flag is full of stars,' " said the third, quoting Van Dyke's old poem.

My mind was beginning to work. Good old Hank Van Dyke, I remembered. He worked for the State Department too.

"E pluribus unum!" announced the first, holding up the loving-cup.

"Annuit coeptis!" I suggested. "He approveth beginnings." But that went past them. Evidently they knew only one side of the Great Seal.

I checked over in my mind to make sure. *E pluribus unum*, 13 letters. *Annuit coeptis*, 13 letters. The simple symbolism of the Founding Fathers. Gosh, even *Congressional*, 13 letters.

"Haven't you forgotten the 13 arrows in the other claw?" I asked. "An eagle can't fly on one claw. Let's have a round of stingers to symbolize the arrows."

"No, no," they insisted. "That's included in the 49. By numerology 49 is 13, 4 plus 9."

"Besides," said one of them, finishing off the big goblet, "we're *pau*."

They paid their check and returned to the chair car. I could see them whispering together as though remarking that they had talked too much. I remembered that *pau* is good Hawaiian for I'm finished, I'm pooped, I'm through.

I called up my broker the first thing next morning.

"Take an order," I said, "and keep it quiet. Buy me all you can, maybe 1000 shares, of American Banner & Bunting."

"Dove, you're crazy," he protested. "The flag business is way down since the War stopped."

"I ran into a bunch of lobbyists on the train," I said. "Big symbol and emblem men. I figure it's all set up in Congress, Hawaii's going to be a State. Every institution, every patriot, will have to have the new flag, with 49 stars. I'm going to be Baby Bunting, right in the fiscal cradle."

"Guess you've got something," he admitted. "A whole new spangle. Hitch your wagon to a spangle. How will they arrange it on the flag? Seven 7's instead of six 8's?"

So I wasn't wasting my time sitting in the State Department studying the olives and arrows and things on the Great Seal. I never waste my time.

State of Hawaii, 13 letters. Aloha nui nui!

Alaska next?

Murder in Red and Green

(PLEASE NOTE, FOR REASONS OF NATIONAL SECURITY, ALL TECHNICAL TERMS ARE INTENTIONALLY SCRAMBLED.)

"WHAT WERE YOU DOING ON AUGUST FIRST, 1944?" SHOUTED the investigator above a levelled finger.

Dove Dulcet, like many others, was accused of having had secret dealings with Soviet agents; as of course he had. It was part of his job in Navy Intelligence to get as friendly as possible with foreign spies. Particularly (this was just his luck) with the only one who could be accurately classified YBB, Young, Beautiful, and Blonde. But (I was his attorney) I was sorry the matter came up in congressional inquiry; I knew he had committed his crime with sincere reluctance.

The circumstances were sinister. When Dove was noticed, in Navy uniform, hanging around arterial crossroads and barbecues in Tennessee, and using the Great Smoky Mountains as a smoke screen, people thought at first he was just a Commander on leave and sitting out a hangover. But he carried a copy of *The New Masses* in his pocket (contrary to all Navy

121

etiquette) and kept asking, "Which road do I take for Bering Straits?" Some smart fellow tipped off the investigators. Another suspicious feature—some of Dove's stratagems always seemed to me a little too naïve—the green on his gold stripes was not the oxidization of deep Pacific salt, but only green chalk.

"What were you doing on August first, 1944?" repeated the chairman. That sort of question can be difficult, but Dove did not falter.

"First I paid the rent, very extortionate, for my apartment in Washington," said Dulcet. "August first is Lammas Tide, Scotch quarter-day. On that date people of Scots descent always pay their rent, and with what is left over they buy whiskey. My grandmother was a MacDouce."

"Contempt of Congress," muttered some of the listening committee, but the chairman knew that the more testimony he could get from Dove the more crackle there would be in the headlines when secrecy broke.

"What were you doing that might concern the present inquiry?"

Dove had been briefed by the F.B.I., and all the Navy top-hamper, not to tell any more than he absolutely must. His particular shrewdness is to tell the most dangerous matter in such a way that when told no one will take it seriously.

"If I really tell you," he said, "will you believe me?"

"Contempt, contempt!" the infantry of thought kept muttering, but Dove has his private resources of assurance. He was once listed by *Pravda* (or *Tass?*) as one of the most dangerous warmongers in America, and he always has that to fall back on in any loyalty test. You would have to know Dove as I do to realize how comic he is as a warmonger. His only real passion is the *Nonsense Books* of Edward Lear, and keeping dogs away from the railings in front of the White House.

"I remember the date perfectly," he said, "because I had a holiday in the country and saw that the apples were turning from green to red."

"Contempt, contempt!" some of the committee said it aloud this time. But the chairman, an experienced attorney, was more cagey. He was impressed by Dove's cloudy and rolling gaze. He knew, as does everybody in legal business, that the man who looks you piercingly in the eye is usually a dimwit or a faker. The man who is aware of the complexity of truth is bashful and oblique.

"Just bear in mind," said the questioner, "that you are on oath, and whatever you say can be held against you."

"What I said was, Natasha! and she was."

"Was what?"

"Held against me," Dove admitted.

I omit (from the transcript of testimony, various uproars and jealousies uttered in the hearing room.

"Gentlemen," said Dove, "my time is valuable, to me and to the taxpayer. May I be terse? I was loitering, for reasons not of my own but of the United States, on the Blue Ridge highway just below an orchard where the apples were turning. Nadya Angina Natasha, like a character out of Tolstoy, came along in a new yellow sports car. I knew she was coming, I had waited for her, by instruction. She was on her way (pretending to be a moving picture talent scout) to find out which of the bar-and-grills near Oak Ridge had really first-class beer and juke. There are only two ways of getting a scientist to talk: he must have genuinely corny music and good white-collar beer. And we knew that Professor Krokodil, the carefully planted uranium expert, would only give that way. He was on the verge of the final integral in the Great Equation. Everything was packed up and ready to blow, and Professor K. was the only man to whom the final differential logarithm had confided itself.

"I can make my sacrifices for the country as much as anyone else. I knew that when Natasha saw a Naval officer, dusty from the road and green with salt, on a country hillside, so far from vodka and chiffon underwear, she would be curious. In Russia the tradition is that all naval officers are grand-somethings of Grand Dukes (or Jukes). I knew that Professor Krokodil (I shan't tell you his real name, poor fellow he was so crazy about his Equation that if you played "Looking Over a 4-Leaf Clover" he'd tell you about it) would be ruined if he ever met up with this kremlinette.

"Gentlemen, assuming you are, don't ask me to be specific. We met there, in the Great Smokies on Pillicock Hill (not very far from Oak Ridge), and I was able to persuade her to have a hamburger, juke, and beer. I couldn't help being sorry for her when she showed me her road map, put out by Esso Marketers, which the Politburo had given her as a prognosis of World War III. Oak Ridge, of course, wasn't even marked.

"I always think it's such a mistake to harry the Soviet agents in this country, they are so innocently useful. They believe everything they read in the papers; they have unlimited funds and can buy new cars straight off the assembly line, and then think they can pass as plain American citizens. Natasha had been raised from puberty (which came early) in Brooklyn, so she had an accent that filling stations accepted as *echt* United Nations."

"Contempt of Congress," someone kept groaning, but now

Dove had infiltrated a romantic interest the rest of the committee urged him to continue.

"I don't want to embarrass the committee," said Dove (the old scoundrel). "I feel guilty of taking advantage of your patriotic zeal."

"The witness will proceed," said the chairman.

"Please don't quote me," said Dove, "or *Pravda* or the Politburo or someone will make capital of it. But my service works on the principle that the United States will never win a war on its own merits, but by the gorgeous stupidity of its enemies."

"Strike that out," said the chairman. "National Security."

I saw the stenotypers cancelling their rolls of tape, but I myself never have to cancel anything; I just remember it. Dove was relieved, I noticed that the pearls of sweat on his bald skull evaporated. He felt easier, evidently, to suggest the roadside romance.

"I persuaded her," he said, "that since we had met beside an apple orchard, we were just a cartoon of the Garden of Eden. She had been raised in the Marxist agnosticism, so she had never heard of the Garden of Eden, but I gave her an explanation that satisfied her. I think I sold the serpent a bit short. But anyhow."

"Contempt, contempt," some of the committee still muttered, but one Congressman whispered that there was a Bible at the Carlton Hotel and he would check up on it. It's curious that except in the Southwest no Congressman understands allusions to Holy Writ? How they spend their spare time must be a mystery to their families. What an experience, to be the family of a Congressman who has spare time?

"Natasha got to be quite frank, or gave the appearance of frankness. I told her, of course, I was a deserter from the Navy and was bearing straight toward Bering Straits. She said she must push on, she had an appointment near Oak Ridge, if she could find where that was, but I held her back as long as I could. I said I didn't like to think of a YBB driving alone through those Tennessee barbecues, but she said she would be on the Arterial Highway in five miles. I gave her one more beer, and doctored it while she was powdering, and let her go.

"It was a sad coincidence, gentlemen. She coincided with that night's big convoy of uranium trucks on Highway Number Nevermind. She drove right into a great van of fissionable ore, and was blotted out like the Duma. (Not even the Russkies remember the Duma).

"That was how the most dangerous, and the only really attractive, Soviet Agent in this country perished. I saw to it that she was reverently buried (not far from that traffic light where she died), and I always put flowers on the shallow mound when the apple season comes."

The investigator had been very patient. "Thank you, Mr. Dulcet, for your candor. We will take everything you have said under advisement. If we decide the country's interest infers us to blacken your private reputation, you will understand our patterotic motives. But still I am puzzled, what did the apple orchard have to do with all this rigmarole?"

Dove Dulcet, even under oath, finds it difficult to tell the truth. He knows how various and mutable (like a beautiful Russian woman) the truth can be; and he knows how Truth, the naked and shining goddess, relucts to be revealed.

"I beg you, gentlemen, keep this restricted," he pleaded. "I had been in confidential work with Professor Krokodil on his distillate of chromogenes. It is based on a superflux of chlorophyll, xanthophyll, and pomic acid. It breaks down, for a short while, the chromophores that control the pigments of the ret-

126

ina. We have been able to crystallize it in rudimentary form, but it requires a little fresh apple juice to vivify. Administered thus, it creates color blindness. You think red is green and vice versa. It leaves no trace afterward. I gave poor Natasha an apple to munch, so she drove head-on, at the traffic light, into a vast ore-laden truck.

"I think of her always in the apple season. Gentlemen, even in your political duty, take care of your chromogenes. Don't get your Greens and Reds mixed up."

The Adventure of
Foggy Bottom

YOU MAY BE RIGHT, SAID DOVE DULCET, THE LITERARY DE-
tective. Unifying the armed services may eventually iron out
departmental jealousies. But as a sentimentalist I'm rather sorry
about unification. When I was in Naval Intelligence the best
fun we ever had was spying on the Army. The U.S. could
have the greatest Intelligence Service in the world if we had
time to spy on the enemy instead of on each other. I'm sure the
President, the Chief of Staff, even the Un-American Activities
Committee, never guessed how zealous was our interior recon-
naissance. The only way the Navy or the Army could ever
find out what they needed to know was by mutual espionage.
Of course the Marines and the Air Corps were hopelessly
handicapped. All they had to do was fight.

Obviously we couldn't learn anything through Channels, and
Top Secrets never got to the top. There was a kind of embolism
in the middle (about the grade of Commander or Lieut.-

Colonel) where they didn't trust anything either above or below them. Everything clotted right there. Most of our own Restricted stuff we could only learn by debauching some Englishman to whom it had been told by an American correspondent in London. OPSHAK, that was my superhush project, used to bowl googlies at British Brass who happened to be over here, and feed them whiskey. They couldn't get it at home, and their tolerance was worn thin. Also, you know how goofy the Englishmen were, what with food and nylons and the *New Yorker* ads. You should have seen some of them give when they got away from the Embassy and out to a party in some rebuilt stable in Georgetown.

OPSHAK? Oh, that was just our professional cant. Operation Shakespeare. The good old Swan told all the secrets there are, but in such a cunning literary convention that no one but Lord Bacon guessed them. Don't forget that Shakespeare was a secret agent for the British Navy at the time of the Armada. The Armada was only an armadillo compared to what we were handling, say, about '44.

[*I thought Dove was fouling his anchor a little, so I poured him another splice. He got good holding ground and went on.*]

In Naval Intelligence we were so jealous of the Pentagon— we were sweating it out in those beaverboard sheds on Constitution Avenue—we'd almost sooner defeat the Army than the Nazis or Nips. We thought, when we saw all that shoulder-nickel at the cocktail spots, if we could only lure them inland to Bull Run. But they were running it, full and bye, at the Carlton Bar.

We knew something weird was in the works. But Admiral Leahy would not tell us, because Admiral King wouldn't tell Leahy. We planted a Navy captain to wear chickenguts for Eisenhower, but he had succumbed to Ike's Kansas charm and was in stays. Nimitz and Halsey and Spruance were too busy to be told anything. We set some very keen Australians to tail MacArthur, but whenever they asked Mac questions he couldn't understand their accent. We smuggled dictaphones into the offices of the news-magazines; but they were so curt, clear, concise (and inverted) we couldn't break the code. There we were, fighting to have a chance to fight, but nobody trusted the Intelligence. We even cultivated some of the Cabinet, hoping to winnow a little chaff. They were pathetically grateful, but they were so busy keeping diaries they didn't know what was happening.

Very likely the Secretary remembers what Bagehot said of Hartley Coleridge. "His excessive sense of the ludicrous unfitted him for official position." That's probably why the Navy and I parted company. I'll never be invited again.

And the only time OPSHAK was on the edge of a real strike (repeat, Real Strike) we were blasted by tragedy.

2.

I had a smart little confidential staff, headed by Lionel Nightwork—you remember him? Brother of Jinny Nightwork. We had inveigled Jinny and her friend Irene Hargreave into the Waves, so they could fox out a certain amount of dope from those masses of mimeograph. It was Lionel who discovered, from a real estate agent who rented an apartment on Connecticut Avenue to an Admiral who hadn't yet paid for his Big Stripe, the Navy's Secret: Put everything dangerous in mimeograph, because no one has time to read it. This agitated Admiral had just hoisted his Broad Pennant over a new flotilla of filing cases, and was a little paper-happy.

Lionel rushed into my office one afternoon. He had been at the airport; I used to send him there disguised as a ground-crew mechanic, to pretend to tinker round incoming priority ships. Actually he eavesdropped the first remarks made by arriving officers. Often they're well fouled up by the long flight and let out something significant.

"There's a priceless old fishball just in from the Elderly Country," Lionel exclaimed. "If Blimp had grandsons, he's one. He must know something terrific or he wouldn't put on such an act. He comes roaring out from the plane, pips and swagger-stick and British Warm. 'America!' he shouts. 'God Bless Terra Firma! Your jolly old pilot nearly did a wizard prang off Labrador. Stoutfella. What price a whisky-peg? I've been sitting in a bucket all the way from Shannon. Now let me put my head in one. Moel Famma!' "

Only the Welshmen there would have known what *Moel Famma* means, and there weren't any Welshmen there. But it's our business in Navy Intelligence to know the expletives of all nations.

"He was travelling High Anonymous," Lionel continued, "but I got his name off his dispatch case, Colonel ffrogg-Bottington. He was met by one of those smoothies from State; you know how embarrassed they are by anything vehement. But the Colonel put us at our ease at once. We should have had a gout-stool for him, but we picked him up at the bottom of the steps and he bade us Carry On. He said he had a whacking great Gladstone Bag; that baffled the State Department. I found it for him and he gave me half a crown; just as if he'd been the Labour Government giving away India."

He sounds to me, I said, like a Cravat of the Old School.

"The old school," said Lionel, "was probably Stonehenge.

You better take over, Chief. He's definitely wizard. He can put you in your place so you like staying there and wouldn't dream to climb out. I heard him speak of the Pentagon as a sturdy little wigwam. Anyone who buffoons like that gives me overtones of suspicion. I think you should track him down."

No can do, I said. I've just got the first thousand pages of Mr. Morningdew's Diary lifted from Treasury files, and I must analyze them tonight. I doubt, and so does the publisher, if there's anything very important. Mr. Morningdew was too hopeful to be a historian; but I might brighten up his prose a little. No, this is on you, Lionel. Trace Colonel Foggy Bottom to the Carlton, give him the old Taj-Mahal, tell him you're a good will-wallah, and invite him out to Jinny's dump in Georgetown. You know the code: tell him it's *burra-pegs* for a *pukka-sahib*, and *chota hazri* to follow. Tell the gals not to get sore if he calls them Wrens, or even memsahibs. Ply him soft-shell crabs and apologize how amateurish we are. Have Jinny or Irene offer to do his laundry. Ask if he wants Sweet or Savoury. Cut down as much as you can on your vowels. Give him a *sola topi*, a *puggaree*, and a *cummerbund*. Above all, hot water in a tin hip-bath and a clean pair of shorts. Give an Englishman hot water and a pair of shorts and he's yours.

I blame myself bitterly, Dove said. (He surmounted a small ventral disturbance.) I had forgotten that Lionel can't drink. He can't coax anyone else to get fried without frying himself. That's something we had to learn in OPSHAK. You mustn't hire historians who love History. You mustn't hire drinkers who love Drink.

But Lionel did exactly what I told him. He kidnapped Colonel Foggy Bottom away from the State Department man, who loathed the Carlton Bar and wanted to get home to his well-bred glass of all-purpose sherry in Protocol Park. He taxied Foggy out to Georgetown where Jinny and Irene had fixed up their virgin quarters. They straightened the candles (which make U-turns in hot weather), unloaded their Chihuahua dogs on the people downstairs, pushed their private mending under their innocent double-couch, and secured the rubber ballcock in the toilet so it wouldn't rumble. They're smart girls, and well-trained in Navregs. They got out their *International Cook Book* (one of our most useful weapons in OPSHAK) and stirred up a smashing kedgeree, with sesamum seeds and chutney and split pulse and those little transparent toasted wafers, *poppadums*. They had everything to remind any pukka pandit of the Sepoy Mutiny. Jinna or Nehru would have been absolutely choused.

It was good teamwork. They made salaam, offered to pay the taxi-wallah, called the Colonel *Huzoor*, and spread him little triangles of anchovy toast and even mustard-and-cress sandwiches. It might have been officers' mess at Sandhurst. They poured him incredible pegs of whisky and cried Here's Lucknow!

You're too Middle-West, said Dove, to guess what that sort of routine does to an old cavalry subaltern from Bangalore. A veteran of the Queen's Own Hussars! I gather from what the girls told me that Lionel put on the heat like an electric pad. The Colonel was stewed in his own *raj*. Feeling himself among Old Carthusians, he really gave. Nor do I blame him. He was only telling what some Yank had confided in London.

Lionel always checked up with me at breakfast. In my little diggings on Q Street I take red-hot coffee while the morning is still cool.

I could see at once that something was wrong. Lionel's eyes

were injected deep in his head; his scarf not secured in his blouse; he hadn't shaved. He tottered toward my steaming percolator but his hand fluttered like a loose halliard. I pushed him into a chair and poured for him.

Buen Día, I said. (I had been up all night with Mr. Morningdew's Good South American Doctrine.) So is this what Foggy Bottom did to you? I hope you handed him Reciprocal Poop?

"Quite," said Lionel. "Oh, very much quite.—Sorry, Chief, I've still got a King's English hangover.—I floated Foggy back to his berth at four bells this morning. Then I took a powder myself."

He groaned, tried to lift his coffee cup, then put his head down to it and lapped. Poor fellow, he looked ghastly, but I had to question him. "So was the handsome bloater all packed up with hermetic secrecies?"

"He was that," said Lionel. "The gals went after him like a couple of vixens, they cosied him with double Rob Roys and a little sofa-sitting. As per instruction I talked Kipling code. A few *rissaldars* and *dak-bungalows* and *jinrickshas* and he began to transfuse. I knew he was ripe when he came through with the immortal compliment: 'You people don't seem like Americans at all.'

"Boy, he was certainly loaded with the inside-in. Even though he was, as he called it, a little tiddly, he would belay himself somewhat in front of the girls, but after they turned in he whispered everything. I mean everything. Timetables and technologies you wouldn't even dare mention to the C-in-C. I realized if we could use what he told me we could win the War without any Army at all."

Lionel groaned and gasped, panted as though he would faint. I waited for the dread secret.

"I've forgotten every damn thing," he said. "You know what cocktails do to me. When I woke this morning my mind was utterly blank. I can't remember a single solitary fact. Down the drain. Washed out. You'd better court-martial me. Conduct unbecoming an intelligence officer."

There's no such thing, I murmured, but he was weeping with his head on my breakfast.

3.

There was only one thing to do, Dove continued. Reproduce, as near as possible, the conditions of the Georgetown binge. If Lionel were to have exactly the same amount of the same drinks, and the conversation were repeated up to the critical point, and someone were to impersonate Foggy Bottom (it would have to be Me), then perhaps—just perhaps—the great revelation would reappear in poor Lionel's stupefied memory.

I sent him back to his quarters to sleep. I called in the girls, who looked a bit hexed, and explained what we must do. They were to spend the day in writing a script, as accurate as they could remember, of everything that had happened the night before. A complete shooting script, not only dialogue but full stage direction, properties, canapés, drinks, passes, and gestures. They're clever gals (you remember that Irene is a greatniece of Sherlock Holmes) and they did better than I'd have thought possible. I wish that script could be published. Some of Foggy's cracks were wonderful, and when the girls lured him onto Foreign Office limericks——

But what bothered me most was the expense account to pay for such a duplicate supply of intoxicants. Bagehot might have got it through the Paymaster, but I couldn't and in fact it came out of my privy purse. Otherwise there'd have been a Senate investigation.

I'll be brief; it's all too painful.

Lionel had a good rest, and after a raw egg in Worcestershire and a couple of gin fizzes he was pretty near par by six o'clock. He complained of pains in his breast, but his sister poohpoohed it. For me that goes double, she said. She was the one who sat closest to Foggy.

Lionel and I turned up at the girls' place on schedule. I had procured (from our wardrobe department) the proper uniform to simulate Colonel Foggy; and I rouged my face a little to get that curry-and-chutney glow. They handed us each a script, and the same appetisers and snorts they had served before. I sat, as directed in the script, on the sofa with my arms round the girls, but especially Irene, because Jinny was on the side where my glass stood. I admit I was a little embarrassed by some of the corny lines in my rôle; I had to remember that Foggy supposed himself talking to simple colonials who would scarcely understand what he meant. It was being called Wrens —*Jinny Wren* and *Reeny Wren!*—that griped the gals most. There were so many stage directions marked (*Drinks*) or (*Fondles*) I had to check them off with a pencil to be sure I was accurate. The accent wasn't difficult, I fastened a band-aid to my palate so my tongue never touched the roof of my mouth. That gave the burra-sahib effect.

Poor Lionel was superb. He knew, as we others couldn't, how much depended on this experiment. It might make the whole Pentagon Building obsolete. I thought he was rather flushed and jittery, but no wonder.

I won't say we didn't enjoy ourselves, grim as it was. The girls screamed with unscripted mirth at some of my readings.

Of course, we were all getting high. Finally, after innumerable drinks, and too much of that starchy kedgeree, and strips of dead fish called Bombay Duck—all of which they had used to bring Foggy to a climax—we reached this point in the script:

> Girls excuse themselves, extricate from Foggy's embraces; Foggy just escapes getting his fingers caught in the bedroom door. Foggy sighs heavily, gives a last look at some cheesecake pictures in *Life* magazine.
>
> LIONEL (weaving a little): Now we don't have to be so protocol. If it weren't for so much official shirt-stuffing, how much quicker we could——
>
> FOGGY: Old chap, you're wizard. It makes me crackers that we have to bung round hiding things from each other. (Whispers.) Let me tell you something—one of your own burra-sahibs told me this in the comfort station at Sloane Square——

At that instant Lionel tottered. He dropped the bottle (he was just pouring what the script called a *lickure brandy*) and shouted:

"I've got it! I remember—— Oh, my God!——"

He put his hand to his breast, and fell. He breathed heavily, but his lips turned blue and he never spoke again. We got a doctor there in twenty minutes, but Lionel was dead. The doctor said that a man with a heart like that should never have worked in Washington.

Dove Dulcet reflected sadly, and then remarked:

Lionel Nightwork was a martyr to duty; and of course we know now what the intelligence was that killed him. He was the first victim of the atomic bomb.

Conference at Quebec[1]

THIS IS REALLY A PIECE IN HONOR OF THE NUMBER 3 TRAM-way, City of Quebec. Wherever and whenever we wanted to go, from the Liquor Commission store in the Place d'Armes down to our comfortable little hotel in the Basse Ville, Number 3 was prompt and ready. Down St. Louis or up St. John, Number 3 goes trundling on. Nobody thinks of assailing the busy wattman-conducteur every few street corners to ask him how far he's got now. Number 3 will set you down right at the doorway of the Frontenac where you can watch the steel-helmeted provosts saluting with such snap that their hands quiver. You can't get in unless you're official, but you hum to yourself (from "The Gondoliers")

> On every side Field-Marshals gleamed,
> Small beer were Lords-Lieutenant deemed,
> With Admirals the ocean teemed
> Round Canada's Dominion.

[1]Copyright, 1944, by Saturday Review Associates, Inc.

Anyway you can look in through the open windows of the Frontenac's big basement laundry and speculate whose undershirts and slips those are. Official linen was running short by then, and I was amused to see Mr. Morgenthau go by carrying a cardboard box that looked as though it contained a clean shirt—unless it was income tax returns, for the date was exactly September 15.

Life continues, even during an international conference, and I was sorry for the correspondents who supposed they had nothing to write about. It would be easy to fabricate a picturesque antithesis: Churchill and FDR going to ground like moles behind the moats and re-entrants of the Citadel, versus the clear glass windows of the Frontenac coffee shop, converted to press and telegraph office, where unhappy journalists sat before typewriters wondering what they could report. Usually they went back to the Clarendon, the best eating place in Quebec, to exchange speculation and wisecrack. They took in one another's joshing. Or perhaps they caught up on their reading—I saw Mr. Shirer wandering about, looking rather baffled but clutching Lippmann's *U.S. Foreign Policy*. The head waiter at the Clarendon is inclined to be a little high hat (which only a chef has a right to) and we had to take him down a notch. Indignation stimulates even the most sluggish French. As he palavered endlessly with some crony we cried fiercely, *"Vous êtes trop pressé pour soigner les clients, vous?"* He had the grace to be a little ashamed. On a table by the door he keeps a bottle labelled by the famous Chauvenet of Nuits, but it's only a symbol. When I explained to him that I have an old wine tariff autographed by M. Chauvenet himself, and memories of the Hotel de la Poste in Beaune, he brought out some excellent Australian Burgundy (Emu brand, from

Morphett Vale, South Australia). Australia seems to be getting around, for my companion Bill Hall, zealot for international trade, learned from a fur merchant that Canada now imports wallabies to be dyed and sold as beaver. He was also tickled to find, in a gift shop specializing in Quebec *habitant* wares, mahogany dishes from Haiti.

At first I was inclined to think that the correspondents were wasting time and expense money by being there at all. Then a sagacious Canadian journalist suggested that these affairs are really, for the press, a kind of trade convention. They get to know one another and exchange confidential humors and anxieties. What idealists and rainbow chasers they are too, always earnestly believing that some terrific story will break; but how meagre are those dim purple mimeograph handouts. Maybe a list of guests at the dinner party given by the Governor General and the Princess Alice; or the broadcasts by Mrs. Roosevelt and Mrs. Churchill. The ladies did their best: Mrs. Roosevelt had a hair-do, which was good for a local story: but even they must have been starved for news, for Mrs. Churchill was seen earnestly scanning the bulletins in front of a Quebec newspaper office.

The press conscientiously desires to be educated, one commentator told me, but is given very little chance. "I'm running with my tongue hanging out," he said, "trying to catch up on what was actually happening two or three years ago." I can't think that this problem will ever be solved, and my own theory is that the really significant news transpires mostly by accident, overtone, humble analogy, and parable. You can't possibly get facts, but you can get feelings. How sardonically apropos of Quebec province's much discussed isolationism was a sentence on the Canada Steamship Line's menu card—it greatly pleased a Raw Deal editor who saw it—"the early French settlers who, seeking surcease from Europe's troubles, followed Jacques Cartier to the New World." And here, exclaimed the gloomy editor, is Churchill landing at Wolfe's Cove to lay those same troubles right in their lap.

I don't myself agree with that viewpoint, but I've got time to listen to them all and no story to get on the wires. I thought that even Mackenzie King looked a little anxious when Churchill said how much he looked forward to fighting all the way across the Pacific alongside the Canadians. The only kind of reporting I reproach is that which deliberately gives a false impression. One famous journalist wrote of "the festooned turrets of the Citadel," but the Citadel has no turrets. The only festooning was the long trails of wire draped round the Chateau for the newsmen's own use. I have no particular resentment of privacy since I cherish my own; even in so small an affair as the choice of the Book-of-the-Month our committee has learned how necessary it is to safeguard its discussions. It seemed to me that when the time came for Roosevelt and Churchill to talk to the press they managed to say nothing with great skill and charm. I thought them wrong in using so cheery a tone (the shocking mob-scene in Rome a few days later gives a warning of the sort of thing that can happen). I wasn't more than ten or twelve feet away (on cramped knees; reporters have to kneel or squat so the photographers can shoot over them) and I think I'm an accurate watcher. One story said that at a good point in Churchill's talk Mrs. Churchill gave him a wifely nudge on the knee. I was there and it simply didn't happen. Another said that FDR spoke with "finger-stabbing emphasis." Not so. He spoke very quietly indeed, like a man mortally tired. Churchill was wearing zoot-boots with zippers. I hope they work, otherwise he'll die, as he should, with them on. I was staggered when the *Montreal Standard's* reporter wrote that they "looked well and rested."

Henry J. Taylor (of Scripps-Howard) was I think the only correspondent who tried, within the limitations of convention, to suggest the physical truth. Even Churchill, the imp of destiny, looked a bit bloodshot from late sitting. But true parliamentarian that he is, he warmed to his instinctive rhetoric: one of those four-part climaxes which no one quoted correctly, nor can I, for I made no notes. I was afraid to reach into my pocket for my pencil, for the redcoat Canadian M.P. just behind the P.M. kept his eyes fiercely on me (the only beard there, and looking very Trotsky). But I grinned appreciatively at the sequence, and Mrs. Churchill, through bright blue sunglasses (I must have looked to her like Bluebeard), exchanged a twinkle with me as Winnie said, of last year's Quebec meeting, "What was then in the egg is now on the hoof, what was then only a sprout has grown to be a mighty plant, what was then mere design has grown to be a mortal blow." There was a quaternion clause, but I've forgotten it; and so has he. I'm on their side, both of them; brave men, doing their damnedest. Which reminds me, more permanent news than any that came out of Quebec was a meeting, held over the telephone across wires down by hurricane, of the Book-of-the-Month Club. Ernie Pyle's account of the American share in the Invasion was chosen, a book called *Brave Men*. It is part of our national record.

And even during a Conference life goes on. I was walking outside the Citadel and heard children in a schoolhouse reciting in unison. I peered through the window (briefly, not to embarrass the pretty young mistress) and this is what they were chanting, I suppose from some Canadian classic:[2]

> Only the busy beetle
> Tap-tapping in the wall;
> Only from the forest
> The screech-owls call.

Roosevelt and Churchill, God help them, were the busy beetles. The correspondents were the screech-owls.

It's queer, you meet a pleasant fellow in the Clarendon or St. Louis Hotel, he admits he knows no more than you do about what's happening, but when you read his dispatch in one of the papers a couple of days later you're astounded how much Inside Dope he seems to have acquired. No wonder there are those great mountains of pulpwood at the mouth of the St. Charles River. They'll be helpful in the waste paper collection a few weeks hence. But it seems a roundabout way of helping the waste paper drive—just as Montmorency Falls is a Rube Goldberg sort of device to provide a suicide club for butterflies. Sitting on a rock near the foot of the falls, I saw four of them flutter too close and get sucked in by the draught. What the guide books always insist is that Montmorency is 100 or so feet higher than Niagara, but more to my pleasure was to remember (perhaps reminded by the butterflies) that Keats had mentioned it. I wonder how he heard about it? See *Sleep and Poetry*, 85–89:

> Stop and consider! Life is but a day. . . .
> A poor Indian's sleep
> While his boat hastens to the monstrous steep
> Of Montmorenci.

[2] I learned later, from a correspondent, that the poem is *Some One*, from *Peacock Pie*, by Walter de la Mare.

I think the most honest method is to give you a précis of a few notes made *au jour le jour*.

SEPTEMBER 10. Waked early on train for customs inspection. Made enthusiastic speech to the officer, saying what pleasure to be in Canada again after all these years. A country truly civilized, I said; soon, after the unkempt litter of Rouse's Point, I shall see the trim lawns and flowerbeds of Montreal West. America, I was about to say, has the *anima naturaliter untidy* (couldn't think of any Latin for *untidy*) but I noticed he looked peevish. "Why are you leaving the United States?" he asked, and I learned he was the U. S. immigration inspector.

SUNDAY MORNING IN MONTREAL: Very peaceful and presbyterian. Scrambled from bathtub three times to watch church parades on Sherbrooke Street, sailors, Wrens and Cwacs. Wrens wear black stockings, Cwacs beige, Air Force girls gray. Odd, this was also the first thing noticed, independently, by my companion Bill Hall.—On Ste. Catherine Street I found a secondhand bookstore open. I bought *The Captain of the Pole Star* (Doyle) for Bill, *Stories by Tchekov* for a daughter, and Guedalla's *Bonnet and Shawl* for myself, total 65c. The bookseller was a Belgian who said my French is very good.

Today's news: Churchill and FDR have arrived in Quebec. Heard a band somewhere playing "The Maple Leaf Forever."

SEPTEMBER 11. Studied the Montreal department stores. Americans are a nation of window-shoppers. Bought some Scotch tartan neckties. At a bank I met a Nova Scotian who said my French is very good. Visited the Osler Library at McGill University, to which Sir William Osler bequeathed his best-loved books. Among many other things (such as the great physician's gold watch that ticked off so many pulses) Dr. W. W. Francis, the curator, showed me the little *Religio Medici* Osler bought as a young student, and the MS. of his unpublished lecture on Walt Whitman. Osler's own suggestion was: "I like to think of my books in an alcove of a fireproof library in some institution that I love; a few easy chairs, and on the mantelpiece an urn with my ashes and my bust or portrait." His ashes are there, and Lady Osler's also, but tactfully concealed behind a panel. Dr. Francis, in a paper read some years ago to the Medical Library Association, gracefully remarked, "That there is no vestige of his brain among the ashes perhaps does not matter since he is surrounded by its products." (The brain was given for study to the Wistar Institute.)

Today's news: Stalin was invited to Quebec but turned it down. Took evening steamer to Quebec. Band played "The Maple Leaf Forever."

SEPTEMBER 12. Beautiful typewriters in the press headquarters at the Frontenac, Remingtons with keyboard including French accents and the British £. At these tempting machines various correspondents sit looking frustrated. Made friends with delightful French-Canadian girl at the soda fountain in our little hotel. She talks no English, but said my French is very good.

News today: the subject of the Conference is choice of supreme command in the Pacific. One expert averred that MacArthur wouldn't get it because both FDR and Churchill are jealous of his prose. This was as much as anyone could learn, so took the steamer up the Saguenay. A rather arrogant priest tried to hook my deck chair. We argued and I insisted it was reserved. I had taken a dislike to him because he smoked cigarettes while reading his breviary, which didn't seem to me canonical? "Vous parlez français?" he asked. "Pas assez pour retenir ma chaise, évidemment," I replied, and he retreated. My brother Felix tells how he once enjoyed a long talk with Lord Bryce, while crossing the Irish Channel, through the accident of having sat unintentionally in Bryce's chair.

SEPTEMBER 13. Even Baedeker gives the Saguenay two stars. Nothing one has heard or read gives any notion of its lonely grandeur. Noble cliffs, frills and jabots of waterfall, schools of white whales. Ideal for a conference, or to consider personal reconversion. Tadoussac a very tempting place.

Back to Quebec in the evening. Stewardess, receiving tip, says my French is very good. (She is from Gaspé.) The news today seems to be that Anthony Eden is arriving with very urgent news for Churchill. Exploring the Basse Ville in the dark, heard a band playing "The Maple Leaf Forever."

SEPTEMBER 14. The look of those handsome typewriters in the press quarters, and most of the time few using them, continues to allure. Say to myself, you can't be a free lance if you don't do some occasional lancing. The news this morning: the Cardinal is leaving for Rome with very urgent news for the Pope. The news this afternoon: anxiety about China. Saw Mr. Churchill twice, driving in an open car with Mackenzie King to the Parliament House. He got enthusiastic reception from the crowds, and looked pink and fit; a cross between a bull terrier and the Cheshire cat. Like the cat, his broad smile seemed to linger even after he had passed. I heard a lady say afterward, it didn't matter now what happened, rain, snow or earthquake, her trip was a success, she had seen Churchill. She shed a few tears of pure Nordic ecstasy. Bill and I also showed our emotion in a way appropriate to ourselves. We decided to collect Churchill's first editions.

The clerk at the hotel desk, when I said I hoped he didn't mind my practising my evil French on him, replied with exquisite urbanity, "Mais pas du tout. Je suis français moi-même." The radio in the hotel lobby was playing "The Maple Leaf Forever."

SEPTEMBER 15. The trim little Canadian corvettes lie in the Bassin Louise, their camouflage patterns doubled in the still water. Behind them is the great silver-grey grain elevator, perhaps really the most beautiful building in Quebec. A marvellous scene for Muirhead Bone to draw. Also the little narrow house, with skew front steps, behind the Ursuline chapel. This we liked so much that one night we slipped a note under the door, expressing our admiration.

I had been reading the French newspapers, which buried the hurricane inside. Consequently a telegram from daughters on Long Island, mysteriously saying, "All safe here. Buildings intact," gave us startled anxiety. This at once took precedence over any kind of international tintamarre, but it wasn't until 3 A.M. the next morning that I could get confirmed reassurance. Those lianas and grapevines of wire festooned on the Frontenac were too crowded with the rumors of the day to leave current for anything else. By the way, the road that goes out to Montmorency and Ste. Anne de Beaupré should be travelled by any journalists who want to make penance. It's called Canardière.

News today: Conference Will Continue Elsewhere. Pacific Plan Now Complete. Embarrassment of Australian Commissioner Who Was Not Invited, Came Anyway, and Was Not Consulted.

Learned that Spencer Wood, frequently mentioned in the

local press, is not a Canadian statesman but the name of the official residence of the Lieutenant Governor. Also that the French word for grapefruit is *pamplemousse*. A Canadian editor who came to dinner told us about a distinguished and witty leader of French nationalism in Quebec (Dr. Hamel) who is a dentist by profession. I did not think in time to say, both dentist and irredentist. Our little Canuck maître d'hôtel mixed cocktails for us, patted me on the shoulder, and said I was *chic garçon*. He added that my French is excellent.

SEPTEMBER 16. Another disappointment for the press. They had looked forward to the following invitation, posted at headquarters: "To All Correspondents: The Boswell Breweries (oldest brewery in Canada) will receive 1–4 Saturday P.M. Vaults will be opened and you be able to enjoy a (or many more) glass of beer." But we learned that the interview with Churchill and Roosevelt had been postponed until 3:30.—Good to know of a Boswell in brewing, as Dr. Johnson was also concerned in that trade.

In the morning I had a pleasant talk, in the sunny prospect of Dufferin Terrace, with a reporter from *L'Action Catholique*. I remarked that within a few yards of where we were sitting there were probably a couple of hundred trained journalists any one of whom could turn out an excellent account in prose of what was happening in Quebec; but to reach the overtones and radiations of the affair would need a poet, or a fabulist like Voltaire. Mentioning Voltaire was a mistake, my interviewer looked grieved—hastily I substituted the first French author I could think of. It happened to be Daudet, and luckily asperged my error. "Daudet!" he exclaimed. "My favorite author, and 'La Dernière Classe' is the best story ever written. I read it always several times a year." Having learned something of French-Canadian sensibilities, I thought this significant.

The news today: FDR and Churchill said that most of the topics discussed in the newspapers hadn't even been mentioned at the Conference. They said so gently enough, and Churchill with gift of impromptu humor. His exclamation "So what?" drew amiable laughter. But I rather suspected they were in for a ribbing sooner or later. The press was not in a happy mood. When they finally reached the Citadel they found that McGill University had stolen the show by a sudden convocation to confer degrees of honor. Trustees and professors and a load of scarlet gowns had been rushed over from Montreal; and while this went on the reporters were hustled and herded down below under a scaffold and among the ancient cannons of the bastion. It was a glorious chance to study one of the most romantic views in the world, but it also looked—scaffold and bastion and velvet pancake caps—like a medieval execution. Looking up from behind and below, one almost expected an ax to fall instead of a silk hood. It is no part of a university's dignity to go touring around to confer degrees; so, at any rate, the newsmen thought. A good press was enormously important, just then, both for the statesmen and the world.—The C.P.R. train carrying the newspaper men home went off the track the next day, and I don't suppose that amused them either.

Late that evening, after dinner at the Clarendon—we knew them well enough now to ask for martinis without those olives of huge displacement. "I hate to remove them," said the thrifty little assistant maître—Dufferin Terrace was dark. The typewriters were deserted, and I trod on something slippery on the boardwalk—a discarded Blaisdell Big Black, the reporters' favorite pencil. The typewriters would go back to Remington, the press and telegraph and censor's desks to coffee (only one cup). In the bandstand they were playing "The Maple Leaf Forever."

SEPTEMBER 17. We were just checking out, and the little demoiselle from the soda and coffee fountain came running into the lobby to say good-bye. She was hastily wiping her damp hand on a napkin; it was deliciously soft and cool as I grasped it. All I could think of to say was, "Votre main, c'est mouillée, très tendre." Courtly as a marquise, she held it high. My French is at least good enough to know what she meant me to do.

On the ship that night (it was the last run of the season) the crew were in excellent humor. The *fille de chambre* said they had made 14,000 beds this summer and now she was going to take to her own for a month. We smuggled some of the last of our Scotch into the dining saloon to give one of the stewards a snort. He comes from Newfoundland, and he said—you know what he said. I didn't sleep very well, because the ship has a broadcasting system that relays whatever is going on in the music room. The amplifier was just outside our cabin window, emitting "The Maple Leaf Forever."

SEPTEMBER 18. So life continues, conference or no conference, and no matter how we sell ourselves short. Tramway number 3 is still running. Little towns along the D. & H. are gay with Monday washlines and phlox and turning sumac. In blue September weather my own beloved Lake Champlain is frothed with a south wind, which means cold water. I never saw Willsboro Bay look more beautiful. The trees are reddening on Split Rock Mountain. The train swings widely over brown highland streams and rocky spurs, and the lady from Peru (N.Y.) who got on at Plattsburg was very unhappy in the diner. She was riding backward; she got very pale and sat miserably afraid of her rich platter of duck. She was much cheered when I offered her 50 cents Canadian (my last Dominion coinage) for her apple pie. She said it would be perfectly good money in Peru, accepted it gladly, and fled the car. That was my congé to Canada.

We got home just before 10 P.M. I had intended to turn on Raymond Swing, to find out (maybe) what really happened at Quebec, but there was the hurricane damage to study. Buildings intact, daughters also, but six big trees down and smaller stuff not yet counted. Yet the most fragile things of all, my blue morning glories, quite unharmed. I don't know why, that seems part of the story.

P.S.—I told a longtime resident of French Canada about "The Maple Leaf Forever." He said he'd never heard of it. I described its lively martial mood. It's certainly not a French anthem, he said. The French-Canadian songs are sad.

Weeding Beets[1]

THE VILLAGE WAS DOUBTFUL ABOUT OUR RED FLAG. AS LONG as we just hung it on one of the beanpoles it wasn't so bad; but this year we put up a staff with halliards. Village officers felt easier when we flew the Stars and Stripes above the other. The only real embarrassment our little commune ever had was when a foreign commercial attaché heard about our experiment in collectivist farming. It was suggested that perhaps the consul would even be pleased to give us a real Soviet flag. We might conceivably get a citation from Big Joe himself. This worried some of the members. In an Old Guard village like ours. . . .

Our red flag is an old mothbitten signal bunting, the B of the maritime code. If you need to know, it was once the third letter of a hoist used as advertisement at a theatre in Hoboken, where it was the final initial in the signal S.O.B.—That didn't

[1]Copyright, 1944, by Saturday Review Associates, Inc.

mean what you suppose; it meant *Star of Bengal*, a play of which the less said the happier. After the opening (and closing) week the producers decided that the letters stood for their favorite Hoboken slogan, *Seacoast of Bohemia.* Nobody stood for the play.

The white initials now sewed on the flag were scissored (by me) from an old undershirt. Even if you can spare an undershirt, that's not an easy job when three of the letters are curly. When the red cloth blows free in our Long Island sirocco, you can read them: R S V P—Roslyn Soviet of Vegetable Producers. An equally good acrostic would have been Churchill's B S T T; for this is our acre of aceldama, our modest community garden where eight suburban families struggle in amateur socialized production. Each member is responsible for certain crops; and on Saturday mornings and Tuesday afternoons you might see one conscript of the glebe creeping on knees and elbows, weeding beets. At this moment there are 800 feet of them that need it. (Our total of beet plantings is about 2200 feet. That's a lot of hands and knees.)

I'd have been grieved if I had known beforehand that the most useful job a world war could find for me would be growing beets. But always self-persuasive, I find the chore has its honest pleasures; even the all-fours posture, which amuses more gracile colleagues, is good for humility and drip. Best are those afternoons when no one else is in the field. The wide sky above is ardent blue and silver (we've had no decent rain for almost a month), the air is julep sweet, and in the herb section (savory, dill, basil, borage) the bees are pushing for place like commuters at a row of phone booths. Neighborhood sounds that would infuriate one at a writing desk are here only a pleasant undertone in the universal diapason.

Dogs bark, chickens crow and gargle, small boys in the adjoining orchard are machine-gunning a beachhead, an Atlantic clipper or a two-tailed Liberator cruises over. From a house near-by comes the palaver of all-day radio. You tie a fresh handkerchief round your brow as absorbent and look hazily to see where you laid down your wet spectacles; or how far ahead along the row did you place pipe and tobacco as lure. Across the parallels of chard or broccoli come tidings of the enormous world. You straighten your acute angles and grunt vertical to listen. It may be Superman or Lone Ranger (bet *they* never sweated like this), or maybe someone's attempt to assassinate Hitler. He was "only singed," you hear; and grunt again as you resume weed-pulling. In such baked earth not even the trick of twisting will drag out those rubbery stems—is it purslane? Wonderful how in early growth it looks almost exactly like the infant beet. You nearly find yourself thinking analogies; but not quite. In glowing utility and sweat you are at ease, rid of the infernal obbligato of thought. Small things delight. Just to discover and rescue one baby plant overgrown by upas weeds is achievement; more than Hitler accomplished. To tear up one of your own seedlings by accident makes you bay with anguish. But mostly you crawl in peaceful stew and stupor. Some tag or tune that comes chancey to mind will keep you happy for an hour. You repeat it a hundred times over. "What stained glass window could repeat The red-veined leafage of the beet?"—"Our vegetable love shall grow Vaster than empires and more slow." Tenderly you succor a stripling from lush vandal stalks; gaze with parent's eye upon its threadlike vein of crimson juice. "If you're ever in a jam, Here I am." That sets you on a new tune for the next fifty yards.

There is comedy too; you're glad no one is there to see. Too lazy to travel all the way to the faucet to turn off the water, you try to skip in between the twirling sprays of our big sprinkler, Lady Precious Stream. She has two nozzles, rotating slowly, but faster than you think. It's possible, leaping across the rows of plants, to bisect the angle, skirmish in between the two jets, firmly grab the arm, and hold it sideways while you lift the heavy standard and stumble muddily elsewhere. But watching to prevent the hose from crushing your colleague's carrots, one spout wriggles free. You get it straight in the face; or worse, on the breast pocket where is your pack of cigarettes. After cannily moving the thing to another parched area you try to rush away. Just then the neighbor (whose water we rent) turns off a flowing faucet. The pressure speeds up, you receive an icy douche on the back of the neck.

Saturdays, when a whole dozen or more commissars are at work together, are more sociably humorous. The promiscuity of garb is a joy to the eye. The ladies particularly, in their wide straw hats and varying lengths of pantaloon or rondure of halter, seem to me to have a Korean look. Some are accompanied by small children who trot with docility but endless question up and down between the rows. Gigantic Simon Legree, chief commissar, stripped to the waist and bawling unexpected madrigals, strides furiously across and across with his hand plow. Not for him the bent crawl of the helot. He has blueprints and graphs of every crop, and regards a failure of rainfall as wanton breakdown of celestial efficiency. I enjoy speculating what these colleagues may be thinking as they apply themselves to their picturesque tasks. They include an architect, a newspaper man, a professor, a publisher, stockbroker, an industrial engineer. In a group so diverse anything might be thought. One of my own anesthetic notions is a kind of Montague James spook story. In an innocent group of suburban gardeners someone, while planting, must have been secretly full of sombre and carnal yen. For later, to everyone's horror, among the cool cucumbers or the prim Swiss chard, something dreadful came pushing up—something so ghastly, so appalling, so gross and unseemly and outrageous, that its exact nature could never possibly be divulged, only shudderingly hinted. On a night of pure midsummer moon a committee of the older men had to go privily and dig it out, exorcise and destroy it—but it shrieked as it was torn from the soil—and one of the members was found dead in bed the next morning—in the wrong bed—I shall never write the story. I learned long ago how much more fun it is just to imagine things; not write them out for print.

I gave up amusing myself in public when I discovered that no matter what one wrote people always called it Essays. But if I were still doing weekly pieces, beets would provide a good formula for the familiar essay. For instance, they won't grow in an acid soil; and they're 87% water. According to the excellent *Pocket Book of Vegetable Gardening* (my reference library in agriculture) their carbohydrate content, I suppose that means starch and sugar, is moderate, only 9.6%. They are 1.6% protein, which isn't bad either for a vegetable or an essay; 1/10 of 1 percent fat, and only 9/10,000 of 1 percent iron. (Every essayist needs to be careful of irony. Look what happened to Colby and Firkins.) They (I mean beets) are plus on riboflavin, and I don't need to tell you how good the tops are as boiled greens. Beets transplant well, just like essays: I've seen an essay transplanted into dozens of textbooks, where the consumer had no notion what volume it came from originally. And, like a lot of good stuff, they started around the Mediterranean about 2000 years ago.

When I first sent pieces to *The Saturday Review,* twenty years ago, I was writing from Normandy; as a matter of fact I was the first American, until lately, who ever spent as long as two weeks in the town of Cherbourg. I was telling you then all about the things that have become so tragically News this summer; for instance the hedges of the Cotentin, and the weather. Don't believe the papers when they keep telling you that June 1944 in Normandy was exceptional. Summer in Normandy was always like that. Ernie Pyle was pleased to find in Barneville the one person (a schoolteacher) who could talk English. I think it was I who taught it to her. I wish I could write you something here that would be as incredibly apropos twenty years hence as those Bowling Greens of 1924 are now. If anyone in 1964 should turn back to the files what could he find that might have meaning? Will there still be a *Saturday Review of Literature?* A Book of the Month? *Pocket Books?* An International Police? Anyway, there'll still be beets.

In the felicity of not writing by duress any more, a grown man puts some of his private meditation into verse; a good deal of which he has no intention of publishing. I think sometimes of that graceful little poem by Cowper about the time when he went to his desk at Olney to do a stint of writing and found his inkwell had been dried up by the sun. He consoled his annoyance by thinking that the unused ink, drawn into atmosphere, might atomize with other moistures to be part of a rainbow. It can do no harm to think the same about our own secret stuff. It may become, somehow, part of the climate. Anyone who wrote to strict schedule, whether daily or weekly, for twenty-one years, has learned a healthy aversion from anything that must be done on time. With what joy, then, he mumbles runes of his own for himself, caring little whether anyone hears or not. I'll tell you one of them:—

> What did you do in man's worst winter?
>> Navigate ships through gale and fog?
> *I read proof for a bloody printer,*
>> *And exercised the dog.*
>
> What, then, in the amazing summer?
>> Did you storm a beach? or write like Keats?
> Did you fly the ocean in a bomber?
>> *I was weeding beets.*

Watson à la Mode[1]

WATSON WAS COUTURIER AT HEART. I DON'T NEED TO REMIND
you that he was first attracted to Mary Morstan because she
was "dainty, well gloved, and dressed in the most perfect
taste." What he admired about her neat tailleur of greyish beige
was that it was "untrimmed and unbraided." He so approved
the small turban "relieved by a suspicion of white feather in
the side" that he watched it from the window as Miss Morstan
went down Baker Street. It was not until a later occasion, when
Mary sat under the lamplight in the basket chair, dressed in
what the Rev. Herrick would have called her "tiffany," that
Watson learned she did the dressmaking in Mrs. Forrester's
household. Shyly he praised the "white diaphanous material,
with a little touch of scarlet at the neck and waist." She replied,
"I made it myself," and what more surely enlists a prudent
man's enthusiasm?

[1]Copyright, 1946, by Ben Abramson.

Watson's detailed description of Miss Mary Sutherland, in *A Case of Identity*, was of course because he was so horrified by her *mauvaise tenue*. The hat was "preposterous," slate-colored straw with a huge red feather; the black jacket was beaded and fringed and had purple plush at the neck and sleeves; the fur boa and muff[2] were undoubtedly scraggly. The grey gloves were worn through. The dress (above the unmated shoes) was a "brown darker than coffee." Darker than Mrs. Hudson's coffee does that mean, implying that it was not brewed strong enough for Watson's taste? Anyhow poor Miss Sutherland's costume horrified Watson's taste in millinery and mode. It was a taste keenly trained at that time, for he had not long been married.

As far back as *Silver Blaze* (1881) Watson became aware of the financial possibilities of the dressmaking business. He made no special comment at the time on Mme. Lesurier's bill, which included an item of 22 guineas for a single costume, the "dove-colored silk with ostrich feather trimming" for Straker's fancy lady, but we may be sure he made a mental note. In the early cases we hear little of falbalas and fanfreluches; even poor Helen Stoner's frill of black lace was not mentioned as glamour, but because it hid the five livid bruises on her wrist. But see, after the meeting with Mary Morstan, how much more technical, realistic (even carnal) the Doctor's female observations become. Just for the fun of parallel columns, let us compare a few of Watson's comments with Holmes's more delicate and spiritual remarks about the same clients:

[2]Is not H. W. Bell in error (*Sherlock Holmes and Dr. Watson*, p. 63) in calling them *feather* boa and *feather* muff?

HOLMES	WATSON

(*Irene Adler*)

The daintiest thing under a bonnet. A lovely woman, with a face that a man might die for.	Her superb figure outlined against the lights.

(*Mrs. Neville St. Clair*)

This dear little woman.	A little blonde woman . . . clad in light mousseline de soie, with a touch of fluffy pink chiffon at her neck and wrists . . . her figure outlined against the flood of light.

(*Violet Smith*)

There is a spirituality about the face.	Young and beautiful, tall, graceful, and queenly.

(*Anna Coram*)

Attired like a lady.	At the best she could have never been handsome.

(*Lady Hilda Trelawney Hope*)

The fair sex is your department.	The most lovely woman in London . . . subtle delicate charm, beautiful coloring of that exquisite head . . . white gloves . . . framed for an instant in the open door . . . dwindling froufrou of skirts.

Characteristic of Holmes's comments is his description of Violet de Merville: "a snow image on a mountain; beautiful with ethereal other-world beauty." Typical of Watson is his note on Grace Dunbar: "a brunette, tall, with a noble figure." He liked them framed in doorways, and preferably lit from behind. Certainly Watson would not so often have said, "I have seldom seen," or "One of the most lovely I have have ever seen," unless it was feminine contour that preoccupied him. At the Abbey Grange, Lady Brackenstall elicited his double instinct for both form and garb:—

> I have seldom seen so graceful a figure, so womanly a presence, and so beautiful a face—blonde, golden-haired, blue eyed . . . a loose dressing gown of blue and silver . . . a black sequin-covered dinner dress.

These boudoir details filled Watson's mind so that he apparently gave no medical attention to the hideous plum-colored swelling over one blue eye.

Watson's cotquean regard for galloons and trimmings was more discreet in his own home. Of his wife's friend Mrs. Isa Whitney he only remarks that she was "clad in some dark-coloured stuff." How much livelier when off on the road with Holmes! See Miss Turner of Boscombe Valley: "One of the most lovely young women that I have ever seen in my life . . . violet eyes shining, pink flush, her natural reserve lost." There were moments perhaps when Watson thought that loss of natural female reserve an excellent thing. And was not his special sympathy for bright freckle-faced Violet Hunter because of the unpleasant electric-blue dress (again "a sort of beige") she had to wear?

Watson's silences are sometimes as revealing as anything he says. He was too shrewd to argue against Holmes's frequent foolish complaints that women's motives are inscrutable. The behavior of the woman at Margate who had no powder on her nose (v. *The Adventure of the Second Stain*) would have been no surprise to Watson. If the Doctor had written the story of the Lion's Mane we would surely have seen beautiful Maud Bellamy in clearer circumstance. She had "the soft freshness of the Downlands in her delicate coloring," writes Holmes (in the new vein of sentiment that bees and Sussex inspired), but if only Watson had been there we might at least have seen "a touch of white at the neck and wrists."

Am I too fanciful to think that good old John Hamish Watson was the first Victorian to do justice to the earliest white-collar girls? Do you remember Laura Lyons of Coombe Tracy whose fingers "played nervously over the stops of her Remington typewriter"?[3] Her cheeks were "flushed with the exquisite bloom of the brunette, the dainty pink which lurks at the heart of the sulphur rose." Watson never made more candid confession than then: "I was simply conscious that I was in the presence of a very handsome woman." It was a con-sciousness warmly and widely diffused, and always double, for the creature herself and for her covering. He spoke with equal enthusiasm, at the same time, of Beryl Stapleton "with her per-fect figure and elegant dress."

There are other passages, but I have said enough to remind students of Watson's specific interest in miladiana, "over many nations and three separate continents," a theme which few but Mr. Elmer Davis[4] have ever examined candidly, and which is so murky that it has even led to the gruesome suggestion of Mr. Rex Stout in his atrocious venture "Watson Was a Woman."[5]

[3]*The Hound of the Baskervilles.*
[4]"The Emotional Geology of Baker Street," in *221-B.*
[5]In *Profile by Gaslight*, Simon & Schuster, New York, 1944.

It has glowwormed others into the uxorious theory that Watson was thrice married. My own notion is offered only as a speculum into the unknowable.

Mary Morstan, a clever dressmaker, found time on her hands after she and Watson moved into the house in Paddington. The medical practice was not lucrative (we know that their slavey Mary Jane was of a very humble order), there were no children, and John Hamish ("James") kept up his frequent sorties with Holmes. Watson, with his special interest in dressmaking, encouraged Mary in her ambition to start a little business of her own. The Agra pearls were sufficient capital. Mrs. Cecil Forrester and friends were sure customers, and the business spread. What else was the needlework which Mrs. Watson laid down that evening when her husband, giving his first yawn, heard Kate Whitney at the bell? Begun at home, by '89 or '90 the business needed seamstress help and an atelier. Watson would not wish his friends to know that his wife had gone into trade, so for her business style she adopted some name of fantasy which has not yet been identified. A business directory of London in the early 90's would undoubtedly shew some Mme. Agra, or Mme. Boulangère, or Mme. Medico, or Morstan Styles, *confections de dames*, doing business a little west of the haute couture. The bills were not as steep perhaps as those of Lesurier on Bond Street, but it was a sound middle-class connection. And Watson, though he had countenanced this, was horribly ashamed.[6]

What else would account for the Doctor's contradictory and baffling references? Mary was properly fond of him, but she had her own life to live, without benefit of Sherlock. The "sad

[6]*London of Today*, by C. E. Pascoe, a lively annual handbook, lists in the 1891 edition, among fashionable modistes, *Mme. Oliver Holmes.*

bereavement" to which Watson referred when Holmes came back in '94 was not bereavement by death, but the fact that Mary and he had separated. Divorce, even if desired, was socially impossible in the holy deadlock of those days. Watson, I have pointed out before ("Dr. Watson's Secret," in *221-B*), had a sly ("pawky") camouflage of his own. As time and success went on, Mary wearied of giving her whole time to dressmaking; and Watson, at the age of 50, even grew a little fatigued with Holmes. Watson's so-called second marriage was when he and Mary decided to resume mutual bed and board. So Watson's second wife was actually his first wife; and there never was a third.

Holmes was too genuine a philosopher to have called Watson's first marriage "selfish." He knew it was part of the destiny of average mankind. He did think it selfish when, after ten years of separation, Watson and his wife decided to make a second try. So when John and Mary set up housekeeping afresh in Queen Anne Street about the autumn of 1902, Holmes began looking for property on the Sussex Downs. Mary farmed out the dressmaking business and said she had always wanted to write. Her first (and last) attempt was *The Adventure of the Mazarin Stone*.

Mary Morstan's influence on women's wear was not lost. Morstan Styles (or whatever the trade name was) became a limited company and she and John still drew dividends. In 1914 the Doctor, long relieved of money anxieties, was "still the same blithe boy."[7] The business spread to the U.S. after the First War. How else do you account for *Morstyle Frocks, Inc.*, in the Manhattan telephone book; or *Morston Textiles* (Morstan & Watson), *ibid*.

[7] *His Last Bow.*

In Memoriam

E. V. LUCAS (1868–1938)[1]

E. V. LUCAS WAS AN EXTRAORDINARY MAN. THE MASSIVE shouldering build, the slow sardonic moods, the moist evasive eye, a sort of smoldering grimness (like a cornered bull, a friend once described him) were what might have been expected in a great tycoon, an owner of mines and factories, a disinherited marquis or unexpectedly defeated prizefighter. Some albatross hung round his neck, but no one ever inquired and those who read his light and well bred writings were unlikely to guess the savage quality of the spirit. Like many to whom the emetic epithet "whimsical" has been hastily applied, E. V. was master of protective discoloration. Even his handwriting was a cryptogram. His essays, because they were the merest fooling, will easily be forgotten; not so his incomparable anthologies, guidebooks, and the masterpiece—patiently elaborated through so many years—the *Lives and Letters of Charles and Mary Lamb*.

[1]Copyright, 1938, by Saturday Review Associates, Inc.

166

The old saying would be true in this case: Lucas knew the Lambs better than they knew themselves. Here he found a deep consoling symbolism, in the sister who was intermittently mad and the brother who wore the dreadful mask of comedy. As editor and as understander Lucas was here supreme. Copious industry to assemble was balanced by beautiful terseness of comment; tingling through to the gristle of the situation.

Hepatic in mien, but ecstatic in vitality, loved and feared and marvelled at, master of the unexpected kindliness and the savage phrase, E. V. was a sketch for something very great indeed. He lived hard; punished others as he did himself; to be thought of as a humorist amused him (more than his humor amused his readers) because there is a malicious pleasure in fulfilling simple categories. He was a great business man and (from simple Quaker stock) loved to oscillate from social grade A to very low company indeed. At both ends of the scale he kept his own counsel. Using the word affectionately, he was a perfect snob. He scarcely ever found anyone good enough to confide what he really thought.

Lowering, witty, of power unsuspected by the casual, he would have humphed with cynical amusement at his obits. Only one as lovingly frank as this would have satisfied his savage passion for the actual and the absurd. In the phrase he knew so well, he was an archangel considerably tarnished, but the gold showed through.

HULBERT FOOTNER (1879–1944)[1]

HE WAS ALWAYS KNOWN AS BILL; HIS CHRISM NAME WAS William Hulbert Footner; he was amused when sometimes at

[1]Copyright, 1945, by Gladys Marsh Footner.

a cocktail party someone in a hurry to be intimate would hail him "Hulbert." Lots of things amused him; and he kept his wide grin under cover until there was someone he could split it with. I always thought it characteristic how many times in his stories someone rubs his lips "to conceal a grin"——

I think Bill was pleased by the many times I told him that no living writer had given me such a total of innocent opiate and refuge. One reason why his detective tales have always been for me the perfect laxative is that I usually read them when I should be doing something else. I used to pride myself on having the most complete collections of Footners anywhere; but then I got the bad habit of parcelling them round in different hiding places (so that wherever I might be, there'd be a Footner available for bedtime or the after-lunch siesta). So now I'm not sure which are missing on loan, or which are simply cached in one of my five earth-boxes. But only yesterday, turning through some old papers, I found a letter from Woodrow Wilson, early 1921, thanking me for sending him *The Fugitive Sleuth*. So that's what happened to it! I remember Mr. Wilson, after leaving the White House, telling me he couldn't find enough really readable detective stories. So I sent him my precious *Fugitive Sleuth*. I think (I'm relying only on memory) it was Bill's first detective yarn. I read it in MS, way back about 1916, when I was contact man for Bill at his publishers. He was the first author professionally assigned to me when I started work at Doubleday's, in 1913. We hadn't been doing too well with his early novels of the Canadian Northwest, and Bill wanted to develop a new vein. He wrote *The Fugitive Sleuth* (first a serial in one of the soft-paper magazines) as an experiment. I haven't read it since Woodrow Wilson got my copy, but I think it dealt with Bill's first detective, that delightful young enquiry agent B. Enderby, who had an office somewhere on 34th Street. 34th Street was the great street of glamour in those days; right across from the Hotel Madagascar as Bill always pseudoed the old Waldorf. And a block away was the Vandermeer, which we would recognize as the Vanderbilt. Bill had studied their exits and their entrances, and many a lively chase took place through their lobbies and service stairways.

For a good many years I knew Bill's books better than he did himself. (In the list of titles he set down for *Who's Who in America* he forgot quite a number of them.) I used to embarrass him by pointing out some unconscious mannerisms that he repeated from time to time; or certain stock characters who took part, e.g. the stout man walking up Fifth Avenue with a slapping archfallen behavior of the feet, making more movement than progress. This, I sometimes had a horrid suspicion, was me. I reproached him, he denied it, but retaliated by actually putting me and other friends (by name and in person) in a crime story laid in Hoboken, *The Mystery of the Folded Paper*, 1930. I think that was the first of the Amos Lee Mappin series, which supplanted his superb creation Madame Storey—the "psychological expert, specializing in the feminine." I got very fond of pickwickian little Mr. Mappin after a while, but for my taste there never was any substitution for Mme. Storey. The greatest mystery of all was the vanished and never explained Monsieur Storey. Bill used to promise me he would some day Come Clean about that, but he never did. My own suspicion was that Mr. Mappin was really M. Storey.

What fun Bill had in describing the luxurious living-quarters of Mme. Storey in her maisonette in the East 60's, and Lee Mappin's costly apartment overhanging the East River somewhere in the 50's. When Bill's own budget was a little austere, as a writer's often is, he had special amusement in giving Rosika Storey or Lee Mappin the best of everything.

Footner's first love was the stage. If I remember truly, this may have been because when he came to New York as a boy in his teens (he was Canadian by birth) he lived in a lodging which looked out on the stage-door alley of a famous old theatre on 23rd Street. Then later, when he was doing clerical work in a financial office downtown (I think it was the unforgotten Sterling Debenture Corporation), he lived in a room above a midtown chophouse. When the weather was fine he spent his off-time in a canoe on the North River. I think he remains one of the few who ever amused themselves paddling zig-and-zag across the bows of Atlantic liners and Jersey City ferries. It was symbolic of much in his life; he always deftly steered across and between and among all kinds of heavy craft; smiling his intrepid grin, and having much more fun than they. I think that was in his theatre period, when a vaudeville skit he had written (with quite serious purpose) proved to be a comedy hit because either he, or his Ingenue Lead, stumbled over the sill of the stage door and fell flat on her face at her first entrance. This was at the tryout opening somewhere in Connecticut; it got a big hand, and they shrewdly switched it to farce, and toured it profitably. Then, I don't know how, Bill got a small part—as a matter of fact he doubled as Bassick and Sir Edward Leighton—in the road company of Gillette's dramatization of *Sherlock Holmes*. I think I remember his telling me that at first he was only the Cabman in Act Four, whose only line was "I've got 'er, sir"; which he must have delivered with such power that he was promoted. Bill wrote a number of plays, some produced and some not, but I'm sure his high moment in the theatre was Christmas night 1916 when Elsie Ferguson

opened (at the Hudson) in his *Shirley Kaye* and he and Mrs.
Footner left at the fall of the final curtain for a maternity hospital. Their first child and the critics' notices were published
almost simultaneously.

With unfaltering courage and conscience Uncle Bill (so we
always called him in my family) wrote thirty or so detective
novels because by some odd chance that proved to be a way of
earning a living. It was a market increasingly overcrowded; his
own vein, which underplayed rather than overpushed his
effects, could not possibly become fashionable, and his own sly
social comments were often lost on the Whodunit trade. In
midstream of this hard work he wrote a couple of novels of
entirely different mood; I still think if they had been issued
over a pseudonym they might have had more attentive reception. They are sombre, sardonic, blunt with knowledge of human
trouble. I mean *Antennae*, 1926, and *More Than Bread*, 1938.
They were of great importance to their author, for they gave
him a chance to express certain stoic observations on the human
comedy he had watched unflinchingly. And then, by happy
chance, he gave himself liberty to do something in more personal vein—which was what all who knew him well most
relished. He had done it beautifully in early days, an account
of his explorations in the untrodden space of Northern Canada
(*New Rivers of the North*, 1912). Now, so long later, he wrote
a testament of his love of New York City (*New York, City of
Cities*, 1937) and then his most moving and heart-opening book
about *Charles' Gift* (1939), the love story of his 30-year devotion to an old house on the Western Shore of the Chesapeake.
There, in the mood of intimate confidence that never says too
much, he wrote pages that are perfect and permanent. At
Charles' Gift, one of the most ancient manor houses of Mary-

land, he had found what he needed and what needed him. How delightful it was, when he came to New York for a few days of skirmish among old friends or publishers, to see him retire again to his Chesapeake solitude; where he had his own deep and meditating pleasure thinking it over. And I don't think he ever quite realized the competition among his overworked New York friends to have him with them for an evening of his own candid and understanding talk. How expert he always was in evading what was merely fashionable and getting into a corner with what was true. He had had a full and complete life: his own eras of bohemianism, of adventure, of family devotion, of nose to the grindstone. I remember with gratitude Max Beerbohm's comment, that Footner was the most civilized American he had ever met.

The day I heard of his death I had just brought back, from a cabin on Long Island Sound which Bill himself had often visited, a large weathered Christmas Log I intended to burn for festival. I heard that Bill had gone (suddenly, without long misery, as he would most have wished) and I carried onto the hearth the great oak stump I had chosen. All day and night it glowed, clear and steady and kind, like his own seasoned affection. I kept thinking of it as his memorial.

T. A. DALY (1871–1948)[1]

EVERY AUTUMN A PHILADELPHIA PAPER ASKS ME TO DO "A nice nostalgic piece" about the dear old town. I never had much of an impulse to do so before, but now there is reason; there died in Philadelphia this autumn one of the most natural

[1]Copyright, 1948, by Philadelphia Inquirer, Division of Triangle Publications, Inc.

leprechauns and lyricists she ever had; an artist who in almost any other great city of the world would have been cherished as one of its Stradivarius instruments.

He was a natural wit, a Huck Finn, half bad boy and half Robert Burns (as was Burns) but an artist to his finger-tips— one of which was crooked due to a hot liner which he fielded when he played shortstop at Villanova or Fordham (I forget which). If you want to know a man's temperament, look at his hands. I used to watch those hands, whether crooked round a noggin of whiskey, or rolling a cigarette, or rolling a lyric. The hands I think of were Tom Daly's.

Tom Daly! He used to build spiral patterns in words as his grandfather laid those perfect spirals in brick, building the noble Absecon Lighthouse. When Tom and I used to go down to Atlantic City, to visit our beloved Hawley McLanahan, we always paid a stroll of tribute up the Boardwalk to admire the shaft of that simple-perfect tower. Tom was, and quite right, just as proud that his grandfather laid those bricks as I was that one of my grandfathers had done promotion and publicity work for Charles Dickens in the office of his publishers. The only lost souls are those who have nothing whatever to kindle their needed pride.

Among this city's unpublished manuscripts there is one I wish someone would print; the article Tom Daly wrote, a year or so ago, at my suggestion: the title was either *What Philadelphia Did to Me*, or *How Philadelphia Did for Me*.

Tom was the last of the old-time journalists. He never owned a typewriter; and you can imagine what happened to an ms., in his lovely fluent script of green ink, in an editorial office.

When I took over Tom's old rolltop desk—I wish I knew what happened to it eventually—in the office of a Philadelphia paper, there was still a pint of green ink in a bottle marked "Commercial Fluid."

Tom had more on the ball than most of our popular comedians. He might well have been a profitable novelist, a sparkling dramatist. But what Dr. Johnson called the "disreputable compliances" of those careers bored him.

He preferred to write his personal stint for Philadelphia papers and go home to Wister Woods. He had a big family to support, and a big heart to unburden.

He liked to sit by the old arch-rounded brick fireplace I remember so well on Rubicam Avenue; to enjoy the yells of the seven children, the embraces of the obese airedale, and Nan Daly's succulent and cinnamon deep-dish apple-pie. Or better still, scrapple from the Reading Terminal Market.

In Wister Woods he heard the dawn-song of the thrush which he put into his great lyric of intimate sorrow.

It was perhaps the most beautiful poem written in Philadelphia in this century.

There was only one place, Tom taught me, to get the *echt* Philadelphia scrapple, at that stall in Reading Terminal Market; only one place to get the *pukka* Absecon Salt oysters, at that little green-and-white cellar on Sansom St. (I stole it as the office for my impossible Philadelphia magazine in *Kitty Foyle*.) The places Tom and I used to go 30 years ago are all washed out. I think of Dooner's, of Green's Hotel (for Tom & Jerry) and the Continental (where Abe Lincoln, yes, and Dickens stayed) and Lauber's restaurant, and Bellini's quiet Italian grubstake on South 9th. I think of Leary's—where Tom and I bought, in alternate volumes, almost a whole set of the books of Frank Stockton at 15 cents each, as much as we could afford. There was my first edition of one of the city's most delightful collector's items—Tom's *Canzoni*, set up between the weekly overset of the *Catholic Standard and Times* (1906), beautiful illustrated by John Sloan, as genuine a prize as Burns' Kilmarnock Edition (when Burns thought he was on the way to Philadelphia). It is marked 50 cents in Leary's famous old Phil Warner's blue pencil.

Tom was infuriated when any of his friends wrote any kind of stuff he didn't think they had any business to write. I am grateful he will never see the Philadelphia chapter in my new novel, which I have just finished after eight years of thinking and four years of writing.

That chapter deals with a region of Philadelphia, say 30 years ago, that has never been mentioned in fiction since Edgar Poe, and I prefer even now not to identify it.

You know, of course, that the young Philadelphia writers, mostly from Central High School, came to New York and founded publishing houses (The Modern Library) and distribution channels (the Book-of-the-Month Club) and publicity bravuras (Alec Woollcott) that really moved books to and fro. But the people who stay in Philadelphia are indolent with an enduring idea. All they ever say is, when are you going to write us another *Kitty Foyle?* And now that I have done it, how annoyed they will be.

Ideas are scarce; whether in publishing or in trade. They were never scarce with Tom Daly. You might reprint some of his lovely Christmas poems—e.g., *A Song for December* (his *Selected Poems*, p. 273). It is 42 years since I first heard a public reading of his *Da Leetla Boy* which brought tears to my eyes. It still does. That is what Philadelphia most needs: tears in its eyes. And eyes, socially speaking, to have tears in.

Merry Christmas!

ROBERT CORTES HOLLIDAY (1880–1947)[1]

"Many of us do not have a separate head at all," wrote the author of that brilliant and touching little essay "The Deceased." "We go in a group. . . . Our names are set in caps, and we have a brisk paragraph each. We are arranged alphabetically. We are set in small type with lines following the name line indented. It is difficult for me to tell with certainty, but I think we are set without leads."

So said, long ago, our dear old Robert Cortes Holliday (1880–1947), probably more like Hazlitt in temper and touch and experience than any other journalist of our time. How accurately he forecast for his own old paper—the *Trib.*, of which he was once assistant literary editor—his own obit. This was all I noticed:

> HOLLIDAY—Robert C., passed away in New York City Jan. 1. Services Saturday, 2 P.M., at Hisey and Titus Mortuary, Indianapolis, Burial Crown Hill.

Much could be said, and was frequently said by himself, about Bob Holliday. He had been ill for a long while, but it was characteristic that his Christmas card (only two weeks ago) was an invitation to his old friends to meet him at an East Side grogshop for the performance of traditional rites. This was immediately followed by a postcard saying the invitation was canceled because he was very ill. But I did not know of his death until I got a note this morning from Christopher Kilmer, son of Bob's boyhood and lifelong friend, Joyce Kilmer.

[1]Copyright, 1947, by The New York Tribune, Inc.

176

It would be a great loss if Holliday's racy and original sketches were forgotten. Particularly "Walking-Stick Papers" and "Broome Street Straws" and "Peeps at People" are a fresh, moody, and masterful contribution to the best journalism of New York City. His strokes of apparently casual comedy were always under instinctive control. He was in the arterial highway of journalism at its best, and he knew—so many of the younger crowd don't even guess—who his real masters were: Hazlitt and Borrow, Thackeray and Gissing, Bunner, and (his great admiration among our own sort) Simeon Strunsky. I think one reason for Bob's and my clear affection, through thirty years, was that we knew, and exchanged homage to, our mutual dominies. If there is such a creature as an essayist, Bob was it. His mind calibrated in exactly that frequency. So he is luckier than less tightly modulated receivers, who go sprouting round among every kind of affiche. Bob's mind ran precisely to (say) 1,500 words at a time. If he wrote, or thought, more than that, it was likely to be turkey.

His absurd variety of excitements was a logarithm of his genuinely Bohemian sentiment. He was, like all first-class journalizers, born in the gutter: the most famous gutter in the world, the Fleet Ditch which became Fleet Street. This boy, at the age of sixteen, a champion bicycle rider in Indiana, was by some strange appetite a seed on the wind. Seed never knows where it may fall.

His three happiest almae matres in New York were the Fishing Gazette, the New York Tribune and the New York Times. It was my good fortune, meeting him in a rainstorm at Browne's Chop House in 1917, to tell him that The Bookman needed an editor. He rushed over there, and the weather was so bad that no one else had applied. George Doran took him on.

He used to complain that he never could sleep on the train between New York and Tarkingtonapolis. Both towns meant so much to him, he was torn between two anxieties. This last time he did.

Among many of his courages, he was the only journalist who had the guts to say, and make a good case, that O. Henry was a flop. I didn't agree with him, but I saw what he meant. He took literature seriously. I love the people who do, and I loved him.

Roslyn Heights, N.Y., Jan. 9, 1947.

The Atom Splitter

Walt Whitman used to live over there [Brooklyn] and edit the
Eagle and go swimming in Buttermilk Channel, two points off the
starboard bow of Hank Beecher's church. Once an old Long Island skipper sunk a harpoon into Walt's haunch when he came to
blow, and the poet, snorting and bellowing and spouting verse,
towed the whaler and his vessel clear out to Montauk before he
shook the iron loose.

—Don Marquis, *Prefaces* (1919)

ANYONE SO COSMICALLY CLOUDY, SO ECUMENICALLY VAGUE,
so gigantically effusive as Walt, cannot often be wrong. He is
bound to vaporize into truth at many points. Like *sortes
virgilianae*, you can oracle almost anything out of the *Leaves*
(it occurs to me that Walt and Virgil had some chemical elements in common). In his own words, the sky o'erarches him,

179

he broadcasts doings of the day and night. Take an example of present concern, he says to America (in *Thou Mother with Thy Equal Brood*, 1872):

> Thy soil, thy very subsoil, all upheav'd,
> Thy general inner earth so long so sedulously draped over,
>   now hence for what it is so boldly laid bare,
> Open'd by thee to heaven's light for benefit or bale.

Even *Sortes H. G. Wellsianae* (you may remember that in 1914 H. G. Wells wrote a whole novel about the atomic bomb) could not be more news-angular.

Walt Whitman really did split the human atom, 90 years ago. His neutrons were always sluggish, his temperament perfect uranium ("rare, heavy, grayish") passing into plutonium; the resulting explosion released a latent energy no editor or acolyte has ever been able to explain or control. Many fine minds, as different as Emerson, Henry James, Swinburne, were blown flat in the backdraft. Horace Traubel dug in the crater with solemn awe and salved a whole museum of oddities, both crystals and cinders. I myself, now for 35 years, have hovered on the edges of that vast excavation; often in true piety and ecstasy, often beset with mirth. Some of us have grown a good deal in 35 years, but Walt has grown faster. "He has proved," Mark Van Doren delightfully says, "that he can make his own way in the world."

He is radioactive for comedy as well as beauty and pain. In a long campaign of sniping at the authorities my happiest exploit was to put into a distinguished biographer's head (and book) that Walt's poem *To a Locomotive in Winter* was meant as a symbol of Mrs. Anne Gilchrist. Mrs. Gilchrist, I remind you, was the English woman who travelled to Philadelphia, every hormone on end, to comfort Walt's supposed amativeness. She frightened him into a palsy. It was a sad and ridiculous little episode, managed with genteel delicacy on both sides. But I love to think of my friend Henry Canby visualizing Widow Gilchrist thus:

Thee in thy panoply, thy measur'd dual throbbing and thy beat convulsive,
Thy black cylindric body, thy ponderous side-bars,
Parallel and connecting rods, gyrating at thy sides,
Thy swelling pant and roar, now tapering in the distance,
Thy great protruding headlight,
Thy knitted frame, thy springs and valves . . .
Thy madly-whistled laughter rousing all.

I mention this because if you don't get fun and games out of Walt, as well as the most delicate and sombre music this hemisphere has created, it is not the Whitman I know. The little skit by Don Marquis, quoted at the head of this memo, shows more slice into one side of Whitman bathos than many chapters of critique.

The only way to deal with him—as he repeatedly suggested —is "with reference to ensemble." Mr. Mark Van Doren's recent 'Portable' Whitman (Viking Press) conscientiously tries. Van Doren gives a generous selection of the poems, together with the two theatrical wings or tormentors in which Walt wished them framed. These are the astonishing 1855 preface, and the Backward Glance O'er Travel'd Roads, written in 1888, which the poet called his Right Bower. Van Doren gives us the noble and sadly neglected Democratic Vistas, which unburden deep anxiety and horror of America's flip manners and social cruelties. This is acid and antidote against taking only the humorous or expansive view; this is Whitman, not Walt.

And our Portable Editor also generously includes a handsome choice of the *Specimen Days,* one of the simplest, kindliest, wisest (and humblest) little testaments ever written. I suppose that scattered through the world there must be lovers of *Specimen Days* who have had the catharsis from it that I have always found . . . "Hast Thou, O pellucid, medicine for case like mine?"—but they are too few. Nothing in modern rehabilitation therapy has ever improved on Walt's handbook of private healing. It should be read in every neuro-psychiatric ward. It is perhaps the greatest G.I. book ever written. No one can ever forget Walt's private bathing and exercising in the hollow by Timber Creek. To regain strength he wrestled with a maiden oak-sapling twelve feet tall. With amazon oaks and bluestocking hickories he was never shy.

I always remember with pleasure Walt's account (in the *Specimen Days*) of his last visit to Emerson. The translucent old Brahmin, innocently gaga by then, sat silent and the northern light seems to illuminate him. Walt sat quiet too. He was always terrified by vivacious or allusive palaver; Pete Doyle and Horace Traubel, Little Neck clams or hickory saplings, were the kind of company with whom he could talk. So the well-bred parlor tinkled with Alcotts and Sanborns and teacups while the two old prophets kept mum.

It was an excellent idea of Mr. Van Doren's to put his selection of the poems in chronological order. It gives fresh purview of our "poet of democracy" to find him ignited on his true career by the European turmoils of 1848. This arrangement begins the book with political induction. Whitman had been writing Home Hints and café-society tripe for various papers (he began, really, as a sort of O. O. McIntyre) but now "out of his stale and drowsy lair like lightning he le'pt forth, half startled at himself." So we gain a new and less sentimental notion, that it may have been the socialists of '48, and not the lovely octoroon in New Orleans, who started his atomic fission.

The problem what to include is insoluble for the anthologist of Whitman. Myself, even if I had to cut some of the marvellous *Specimen Days* or the grim *Democratic Vistas*, would have pleaded for *By Blue Ontario's Shore* and *Thou Mother with Thy Equal Brood*. I can't agree with Van Doren that the gist of *Blue Ontario* is communicated in the few lines he quotes in his wise and sensitive introduction. I would regard that poem as a Must, even if only to show how Walt thriftily resumed in it the key passages of the 1855 Preface. What an author takes the trouble to publish twice is important to him. I would have wanted also, if possible, *The Song of the Answerer* and *Starting from Paumanok*, and some of the brief *Inscriptions* which Walt thought of as his advertisement and signal-hoist. But these thoughts I pass by in my grievance that Mr. Van Doren's text of the supreme *Song of Myself* is so unsatisfying. He says in his preface that Walt's revisions are important—and then pays no attention to them. Which of the versions he followed I don't know, but it differs in many places from the unquestionable best and latest. It retains some of the worst of the 1855 juvenilia, e.g. the appalling line

Washes and razors for foofoos—for me freckles and a bristling beard

and the anticlimax about the farmer's girl and her iron tea-kettle. If one retains these comic absurdities they need a footnote to let the reader know Walt was wise enough to delete them later. And (p. 87) there is one grave misprint: *extollers of armies* should be *extollers of amies*, viz girl-friends.

Likewise, the *Song of Occupations* does not include its best and final stanza, the wonderful passage about the nightwatchman's daughter. But maybe I'm prejudiced, because Kitty Foyle's father was a nightwatchman.

There can never be too many collections, recensions, editions of Walt, and I welcome this one as I have welcomed all. Like Lady Mount Temple's red silk knitted waistcoat which she sent to him in Camden, and caused so much nuisance with the Customs, they are all too small for him; but any of them may set off an atomic explosion in some destined accidental reader. They are all "letters from God, dropped in the street." Mr. Van Doren says of the famous Emerson letter, which Walt exultantly quoted on the backstrip of his second edition, that better praise has never been bestowed upon the book in equal space. Oddly enough it has been done by several people: e.g. by Robert Louis Stevenson, by Bliss Perry, and even by myself. The Old Guard don't quite forgive Ralph Waldo for his palinode and recantation. See the letter Emerson wrote Carlyle circa 1856 in which he suggested that if Carlyle didn't like *Leaves of Grass* he might use it to light his pipe; and then again the faintly-praising testimonial that Emerson sent to Salmon P. Chase, in January 1863, when Walt wanted help for a job at the Treasury. Mr. Walt Whitman, said Emerson, has "marked eccentricities"; how's that as a recommendation for a Treasury employee! I turn with gratitude to the payoff saying of the good Bliss Perry which I read as a college boy and which I think first brought Walt home to my own business and bosom:

> Numbers count for nothing, when one is reckoning the audience of a poet, and Whitman's audience will, for natural reasons, be limited to those who have the intellectual

and moral generosity to understand him, and will take the pains to do so. But no American poet now seems more sure to be read, by the fit persons, after one hundred or five hundred years.

To this I always append, in my own mind (a place where many joys are quite secure) Walt's own gorgeous remark about the *Leaves* when John Wanamaker wouldn't sell the book. "If I didn't understand them I wouldn't like them myself."

Any appropriate memo about Walt is likely to be as disorderly as Walt himself; so I may be forgiven for mentioning a concern. Ever since I persuaded Doubleday Page and Company, now Doubleday, to take over the authorized Whitman editions from executors Traubel, Harned and Bucke (that was back in 1917) I have wondered when someone would republish a digest of the incredibly amusing and fertile volumes by Traubel, *With Walt Whitman in Camden*. In all biography there is hardly anything else like them; a dustbin of delight. Logan Pearsall Smith (who used to go over to Camden as a young fellow to pay homage to Walt) would have been the citric aphorist to write a preface. Mr. Van Doren doesn't mention these extraordinary scrapbooks—few people ever do, they simply bag Traubel's stuff. There you see Walt at his ease, dominating his naïf disciples in the hope—"cute" he would call it—that someone else, some day, would tune in. He sat there in his rocking chair, gossiping in the candlelight of old age, chanting the square deific. Not Socrates getting ready for the hemlock was more simply wise and assured. He must have thought ironically of his line that great poets must have great audiences. He had an audience that could swallow camels but didn't know gnats existed. It is still rather like that. They named a hotel for him, and Longines even trademarked a very smart wrist-watch with his name, but they won't read his stuff the way it needs to be read. But he was the Man-o'-War Bird, and he wakes anew on his prodigious pinions. Rarely has so much been done for so many by one divinely blundering man.

Two Tributes

These unstudied homages were written in praise of two of the most perfect artists—in their own skills and variations—we have known in our time. The first was a letter to my old friend W. S. Hall, probably the first collector of Max in the U.S.A., on the occasion of Beerbohm's 70th birthday, in August 1942. The note on Mr. de la Mare was written for the tributary volume (Faber & Faber, London) published in honor of his 75th birthday in 1948.

It is partly egotism, I suppose, to wish to put oneself on record in praise of wordsmen—and draughtsmen—so silky, sober, and serene. If there were not nearly 40 years of devotion behind it, I might hesitate. But there is always the possibility of suggesting to the young Zulu impi, *now so baffled and so periphrast, that neither humor nor horror were unknown before.*

Neither of them (these great eluding conjurers) are likely

187

to see these memos, nor are they intended to see them. They are for the few and freakish readers by accident. Once and half-a-while a new devotee is inoculated by suggestion.

LETTER TO A COLLECTOR ON
MAX BEERBOHM'S BIRTHDAY[1]

OBEYING IMPULSE. AFTER HAVING THOUGHT SO OFTEN ABOUT Max Beerbohm all these months I won't feel easy to my conscience if I don't write you a birthday letter for next Monday (24th). I have a feeling that no two guests at the birthday dinner will be more actually there in feeling than ourselves— and in some ways I'm almost glad not to be there in any carnal form.

One's feeling about Max is a reflex of his own surely and wisely developed delicacy; one keeps it a bit secret to one's self; it is always specially pleasing to me to observe the bewilderment of the non-Maxers or un-Maxed when they happen to overhear two devotees. There can scarcely be any form of more innocent and more honorable snobbery than that private certainty that damn few of this world's unpleasing mammals have the faintest idea who he is, or what he has written and cartooned, and why he did it that way. It is a special flavoring of this snobbery that of all those who have least notion of his quality his American publishers have usually been preeminent—I love to wonder what he would have thought of those unproofread Dodd Mead editions if he ever saw them.

Another feeling that I sometimes enjoy is the realization that his "incomparable" quality was of careful and loitering growth; he was fairly brash when he began; and it charms me

[1]Copyright, 1942, by Saturday Review Associates, Inc.

that he developed to such perfect tone and suggestion that the
errors of some of his earlier pieces only serve to heighten and
freshen one's pleasure in his exquisite masterpieces. One will
always have one's own favorites, and for reasons of one's own;
mine, most likely, is *No. 2, The Pines;* partly because it so
perfectly recalls Victorian interiors I myself have known, and
even a fine old gentleman (Swinburne's contemporary) I used
to call on and listen to his anecdotes of bygone giants. In *No.
2, The Pines,* once you enter the house and sit down to the
mutton (and turnips, I'm sure) with the coal fire behind
you and a glimpse of the garden through the window, and
the "parlourmaid" corset-breathing behind you, and the Ros-
setti ladies in frames on the walls and the enormous big English soup or dessert spoons and the tureens of gravy and the
bread cut in cubical hunches, why you are alive in that particular world that young men like Max, or even younger men
like ourselves, knew something about. I bet there was a monkey-
puzzler-tree somewhere near by; and I suppose the be-*yoo*tiful
babbie A.C.S. saw on the heath was killed in the 1914–18 war.

Well I defy you to reread *No. 2, The Pines* without a small
moistening of the eyes toward the end.

The best way to celebrate (not the word, I fear)—the best
way to meditate Max's 70th would be by silence; those who
don't care or weren't enough interested to inform themselves
simply don't matter. The boys meeting at the dinner table
in London will deservedly cheer themselves with good wine
and good words; but the moment commemorates something
that can hardly be expounded that way. Everyone who has
loved Max's touch has always thought of him as the quintes-
sence of insouciant youngness; of a delicacy of feeling so
tenderly shaded it scarcely admitted itself to itself; a suggestion

of ribaldry so polished and of satire so sharpened that it was only we ourselves, in the kindest and sweetest hours of our own youngness, could have perceived it. We were just enough younger than Max himself to be his perfect audience. Don't I remember buying *Zuleika* in Oxford the very day it went on sale at Blackwell's bookshop: exactly opposite the Roman emperors of stone; I was 21, and I read it sitting on a bench in New College gardens; and of course was hugely amused by the opening and even at 21 I perceived that he had dragged out to great length what should have been only a pastiche. Among the half-educated of N.Y., some ten years later, there was great admiration about *Zuleika;* but no one who ever really knew Oxford thought it was so very amusing. That of course was part of Max's "bad period" (every good artist has to have a so-and-so period)—it's an odd thing that it really took a world convulsion to bring this "petit maître" to his largest creativeness and more generous ardor—He won't approve these words which I'm putting down without even pause to choose carefully; on this hell's own humid evening and with the encouragement of a glass of beer. But you know what I mean: Max's beginnings, however witty and charming, were on the coterie and smarty side of things; it was only later that he became the completely judging and accomplishing satirist, the critic as swordsman.

So wise a creature, I can't believe that he really looks back with regret on his own youth any more than you or I do on ours; *we* may deplore that he is 70, because we fixed him in mind as a star in the clear sky of our own boyishness. And we can curse that the world he knew and adorned with exquisitely intellectual mirth is gone for always. Those who never felt and smiled with him in that world can't possibly do so now; the foundations and catchwords of that laughter are gone. It amuses me no end to think that some of the most richly furnished of modern Beerbohm "collectors" probably don't even know what he's talking about most of the time.

I admit I should like to hear what Jim Bone & Ivor Brown & Philip Guedalla & Raymond Mortimer might say at that dinner. Mortimer was co-author, with the late Hamish Miles, of a spoof about Oxford (*Oxford Circus*) which I always thought was more successful than *Zuleika*. Guedalla, of course, was the Max Beerbohm of Oxford in my day. Ivor Brown, long a contributor to the *Manchester Guardian* and lately appointed editor of *The Observer*, is a brilliant cove; and, like Max, a drama critic. I wish there might have been an American at the meeting, to take up some of Max's hilarious taunts at the U.S. But the particular sense of artistry in which he reared himself, that delicious and temperamental and acid-etched sense of comic form, hardly exists in the U.S. and maybe never will. (Remember his cartoon of Walt, exhorting the American eagle to soar.) So one looks back at Max as one does at some of the old Roman poets, let's say Horace; or Ovid among the Goths; marvelling that the spirit of the arts could stamp such perfect design and harmony on the unpromising base metal of human being. Poor old blighter: he wrote you once that he was enlarging his library (with a Gordon Craig bookplate!)—did he get his stuff away from Rapallo when things blew up?—And how I wish he might have done a cartoon of the incident of you and the lady aboard ship (*S.S. Von Steuben*, was it ? ?)—what a marvellous subject yourself would be for his pencil.

Today, among showers of rain, I reread pages here and

there, I noticed ("Laughter," in *And Even Now*) he protests that even "at the age of 47" he still laughs often and loud and long. Maybe I was morbid about ages, thinking of his septuagint, for I reflected mildly that I myself am now ten years older than Max was when he wrote "No. 2, The Pines."

P.S. Monday, August 17

Another chute of rain came down and I was just too sour to finish. Max in one of his stories describes how bad weather affects him, so he would condone. Besides I was getting ill-humored anyway thinking of the contrast between so much dull, foggy, fumbling, mud-cloyed writing and the stinging precision of Max. Writers without gift, publishers without taste, and ten times ten million readers without sensibility—O Saeclum insipiens et infacetum! And while so many were out in the garden eating worms Max was sprinkling diamond dust.

WALTER DE LA MARE

ANYONE BUT WALTER DE LA MARE WOULD THINK WHAT I AM about to say too personal or too silly. But not he. He knows that part of the triumph of poetry is in its freedom to be as personal, and as silly, as possible.

Tonight, a hot humid midsummer evening, I sent a household (wife, three children, a nephew) out to recover from domestic fatigues by eating dinner at a local tavern. I said I would stay home and mind the grandchild. It so happens that this was my first real experience of babysitting with a grandchild. As soon as his mother and the other practised members had vanished, the babe began to yell, with the fury of 3½ months. It might have been the fact that he has just been promoted from bassinette to crib, or it might have been a twinge of colic; but after letting him roar awhile I scooped him up and walked him and rhythmically thumped his back. Since no one else (but an old hypermaternal spaniel) was in the house, I even sang; never mind what or how. The purport is that, while walking and mumbling and thinking of the pathos of that small helplessness and that bide-its-time possibility, I suddenly thought of Walter de la Mare. All men have thought nobly about infancy, but he is one of the few who have put such thoughts in noble and lasting music. Human speaks to human everywhere and circumvents barriers. I knew, absurd as it looks in the chill of print, that our hero would be pleased that an apprentice gaffer in his agony remembered the deepest spokesman of our guild since Victor Hugo.

A bidding prayer for all such!

I have never been quite the same—not quite so cumbered with mere soil—since first reading *Peacock Pie;* more than a generation ago. I was young and impressionable; now I am elderly and impressionable. If all these years I have been, secretly, scorched and blessed by occasional sense of fancy, it is partly by the encouragement of his demon magic.

Nor have I, for many years, made myself a nuisance to him by telling him my admiration. Americans are mostly more shy than British, and when I was told long ago he could be reached at some Maidenhead number I was too delicate to say it to the telephone lady.

Walter de la Mare is quite outside the purview of casual comment. I have sometimes thought him a little chatty in prose; like the great spirit he so much physically resembles, Charles Lamb. In verse he has the pattern of wind-blown sand. It is always perfect pattern; if the sand is fine and the wind steady the spiral is past soft comprise. He lingers, then, or lapses, between bliss and despair. Perhaps that is the habit of grandfathers? Sometimes he tunes the string intolerably taut; the mind itself becomes hollow shell, twangled with strange overtones. He is the spokesman of the borderlands of feeling.

Who ever grew older so gracefully?

He taught us the sense of horror. Unless himself so simple, so kindly, and so dour, how could he have said such shocking things? I am sorry only for those who were not shocked. Look again, for medicine, in his recent book *The Burning-Glass*.

Grisly old harper! In muted and twilight airs he gives us his miracle. Long ago he passed the gamut of noonday speech. In that unsurpassable melody he is Ariel matured; sunset between the cromlechs of Stonehenge. He is what we in the States would call a hermit thrush, a singer more sweet than your oversold nightingale. He is the lord of semitones.

"Sweep thy faint strings, musician." There are still some who need and deserve such music.

Tempest 1941

A NOTE FOR SHAKESPEARE'S BIRTHDAY

IVORY BOMB–SHELTER

THE RICHEST REVENUE OF ANY ART IS THE UNEARNED INCRE-
ment it sometimes acquires from what happens later, of which
the artist could have no specific foreboding. No matter how
high the intention nothing could be written, *ad hoc*, so moving-
timely to Now as *The Tempest*. There indeed was "a kernel,
sown in the sea to bring forth other islands."

Tempest 1611 was probably taken by many of its earliest
audience as a pleasing waggishness and "quaint device"; though
I can imagine Beaumont and Fletcher going back to their joint
lodging and telling the famous Mutual Wench (see Aubrey)
that Will Had Something There. But the full measure of what
he had needed more than three hundred years to reach its
perfected felicity—or frequency. It had to wait for the invention of radio. I learned only the other day (*Studio* Magazine,
January 1941) that on the façade of Broadcasting House in

¹Copyright, 1941, by Saturday Review Associates, Inc.

London is a beautiful statue of Prospero and Ariel carved by the late Eric Gill.

Through the months of a damned and anxious winter *The Tempest* was my secret resource, my private War Relief. An ivory bomb-shelter, you may suppose; but I found it not a flight from reality, rather a change of venue from one sort of reality to another not less actual; as it perhaps was for Shakespeare himself. I imagined myself a director staging the piece for immediate production, and I dare say I spent more time thinking about it, and transcribing it line for line in an abbreviated and practical script, than its author ever did. The conception of Ariel as an invisible radio-voice makes the fable instantly rational to our own habits of thought. Where Ariel's invisibility requires extra lines for that spirit, it was easy to supply them from the Sonnets, or such a stunning felicity as Glendower's lines (in *1st Henry IV*)—

> The musicians that shall play to thee
> Hang in the air a thousand leagues from hence.

Indeed the analogies became so momentous that, as spring approached, I could think of the play only as *Tempest 1941*. In the queerest way it always kept just ahead of the news. When the lend-lease bill was being argued I found the stage direction *A Ship at Sea; Afterwards an Island* the most literal and brief abstract of the Battle of the Atlantic. When an American luxury liner went mysteriously aground on a Florida sand-bar I thought of course of Shakespeare's bewitched shipload of fascists in the tropics. Whenever I carried firewood from the backyard pile I flattered myself as the "patient log-man"; and Ferdinand and Miranda easily reminded me of the Duke and Duchess of Windsor, also humble refugees from courtly comme-il-faut. I could not even set about any routine job of journalism or lecture without saying grimly to myself, "Let's hang some trumpery on the line." I mention this remark of Prospero's because it was the only speech I was really sorry to lose in my shortened version. I lost it because I felt, at that point, my imagined audience had had all they could endure of Stephano and Trinculo—who were, as Shakespeare's stage direction so far anticipated modern argot, "all wet."

Like everyone else, I guess, I had been thinking of *The Tempest* all these years as a philosophical allegory of the inward self—whether Shakespeare's or anyone's. I said enough about that notion of it in a book published ten years ago (*John Mistletoe*) to go on record, and have no taste to rehash it. But it needed another World War to show how fantastically apropos it is as political fugue. (Rauschning in his latest book *The Redemption of Democracy* has a powerful passage, pp. 98 ff., on the "Calibanism" of the totalized states.) It took the tragic capers of Mussolini, dressed like an organ-grinder's monkey, to lampoon the astonishing parallels. I considered writing a marginal gloss, thinking of Coleridge's glorious argumentation running like the pilot's dory alongside the steep hull of the Ancient Mariner; but indolence persuaded me it would annoy the reader and cause a lot of typesetting trouble. It would begin something like this:—

A ship of state, carrying totalitarian leaders homeward after a politico-social junket in North Africa, is overtaken by sudden gale . . . which drives the vessel upon unknown dangers. . . . The behavior of passengers and seamen to each other at once suggests that this is not just a sea-sorrow but also a political fable. . . . And Miranda's first words enlarge the suspicion. It was a tempest raised by "art"—viz. a brainstorm or a passion in the mind, and its ravages were intellectual. . . . So Miranda, true to her name, is full of wonder. Reared in that innocent isolation, she knows nothing beyond the island; remembers nothing of her infancy save the troop of tirewomen. . . . Of Mrs. Prospero we learn only the unrelished commendation "a piece of virtue." Pushing the heroine's mother out of the story is of course a frequent simplification in fiction; especially when the author favors the idea that a girl raised in a world of men will be cured of female pragmatism and so more lenient to man's goat-caprice. . . . Shakespeare has been accused cynic in his deletion of grown-up women from his most original parable, but "What the Author Had in Mind" is less concern of ours. . . . The question is, What Has the Reader (or Spectator) in Mind? . . . And so Miranda, perhaps because it is the tropical siesta-time just after lunch, finds the Old Man's narrative something drowsy . . . until she herself comes into Prospero's story, which rouses her curiosity at once. . . . On the island that Shakespeare is talking about, the lonely island of the individual mind, that is usually so? Drowsiness toward others' problems, prompt wakefulness when *I* come on the scene. . . .

During those winter days I several times relieved my mind by dictating extempore memoranda about the play. They are not polishable, but they are part of the record and I preserved them as an evidence of the kind of collaborative reading which I think should be encouraged.

COLLABORATION

The good reader collaborates with the author. This morning let's choose a colleague; let's choose Shakespeare.

It's over thirty years, I think, since *The Tempest* was last produced commercially (if that's the word) in New York. If I were a theatrical entrepreneur that is the play I would choose. It isn't even a play in our usual meaning of the word. The title itself is ominous and fearfully of Now. Let us imagine that we know nothing about this script, handed us this morning by our collaborator, and re-examine it according to our own necessity.

"Scene: a ship at sea; afterwards an island." The first question to ask, is this a real ship, is this a real island? Prospero's opening speech gives us our clue. After the storm and shipwreck he tells us, "There's no harm done."Obviously then it is not an actual ship, and the storm is a storm in the mind.

With that clue, then, we consider the first scene. At once we observe that the persons are of two kinds: the dichotomy suggested by Kipling as the Marthas and the Marys. The shipmaster and the bosun are sons of Martha, theirs is the job to navigate the vessel and save her if possible. The sons of Mary are the saloon passengers, a group of fascist aristocrats who swarm up on deck as soon as the ship is in danger and get in the way of the crew. There is some evidence that Shakespeare knew more than a little about ships, and we see at once that his sympathy is with the skipper and the bosun. Plenty of savory details could be noted about this brief little prologue but let us leave it at this: our collaborator begins by suggesting a definite social breach (he even uses that word in regard to the ship, "We split, we split!") between earth's passengers and crew. It is suggested this first time on the lower level of actual handiwork and physical skill. Later he drives this fissure through the world of politics and of intellect itself. I wish there were time to insist upon the technical accuracy of the ship's handling: setting the "main course," for instance, is exactly what would need to be done to claw off a leeward shoal. But in the case of this collaborator we may take it for granted that his technical details are likely to be exact.

Scene 2: Even the most casual reader will notice the allusions to Prospero's "art." A prime purport of our collaboration must therefore be to enquire what is the nature of this art? The simple reader will say at once, oh some kind of magic. Aye, indeed, but for our present significance, what sort of magic? For the concepts of its earliest audience it is a magic which our colleague thought it necessary to symbolize by an actual garment—a "mantle." We ask ourselves, what would a mantle suggest to that audience? A mantle of darkness? A mantle of secrecy or solitude or invisibility? Note that in dealing with this collaborator we need always to ask questions that have two-way stretch. We can best learn what a passage really suggests to us if we can divine something of what it suggested to him.

There comes then somewhat lengthy dialogue between our magician Prospero and his daughter Miranda (and even their names may have meant something special) in which Prospero tells how the scholar who neglected worldly affairs was exiled from his dukedom and how with household goods and books he arrived at this island. Miranda (age 15, remember) rapidly wearies of the story and seems to pay no heed. One of the oddities of this island, frequently mentioned, is the drowsy quality of the air. No nembutal or other soporific is needed for the mind to lapse into dream. So we begin to get a little prickling in our mental thumbs: Good Lord, we say, is this whole scenery laid in some inner and sleepier region of the mind itself? Are these characters symbols of different ways of thinking that emerge only momentarily from an ocean of subconsciousness? So already we are alert to detect what kind of tricks is our collaborator playing. Perhaps the unspoiled young mind of Miranda knows at once that this reminiscence of Naples, Milan, usurping brother, &c., is just the old traditional hooey, the standardized plot which our friend used again and again. And so Miranda is again asleep when a quite new kind of character enters—and enters in a quite different sense: Not to the eye but to the ear.

ENTER ARIEL

"'Tis a good dullness, and give it way," says Prospero—the best advice that can be said to any artist. Each mind has its own variety of dullness and must discover its own mode of refreshment.

There is a drowsy quality (Caliban tells us) in the island air. It is the island of the subconscious where the mind is getting ready to think things that have not yet taken form as words. The visions and sound effects of that island have the same relation to written words that the bee in the hollyhock has to the eventual honeycomb.

The extraordinary excitement of *The Tempest* is that no inquisitive unspoiled mind ever examines it without feeling intuitively, here is something quite outside the rules. It does not know just why or how. Is it just an idiom of my own that my adolescent recurring fancy or deliberate put-myself-to-sleep imagery was of a beach of yellow sand and an always unidentified Miranda in the clear, Bermuda-colored surf?

Collaborating with our partner, as though he had just brought us his manuscript, let's first be a bit literal. What is Ariel "and all his quality"? First he filled the ship with flame and puzzled its company distracted. It sounds, today, like a symbol of the Press. Ariel had formerly been the slave of the damned witch Sycorax, for whose purposes he was "too delicate" and was imprisoned in "a cloven pine"—which we might, for our own humor, identify with any forest of newsprint pulp. (This is no more grotesque than any other commentator's trapeze work.) The spirit Ariel, who had been bewitched into groaning hackwork, was released by Prospero's art into his new airy service. Note even in Prospero's severities to Ariel a feeling of affectionate chaff as of an employer to his most intimate employee. No matter how silly it may seem to hang a placard around Ariel's neck, the collaborating mind may find it useful to do so. What is one secret hope or desire of every magician: to move the minds of innumerable people and so to readjust the great weights and burdens of the earth. Even Dr. Einstein, whom we have long thought of as a modern Prospero, marooned in the intellectual island of the Institute for Advanced Studies, has his own Ariels or associates, and finds the old sweater and pants as necessary to his art as the mantle or dressing-gown, which was evidently Shakespeare's symbol of Professor Prospero's studious isolation.

So we pin on Ariel a tentative label wider than The Press. Let us call that spirit Communication. Perhaps even, using the many suggestions of speed and music and multiformity, let us call him Radio. Even by a lamentable pun, Aerial. It is not impossible that is exactly what Shakespeare meant, though the encyclopaedia contradicts us.

With the simplicity of dramatists our author thinks it necessary to offer the immediate contrast of Ariel and Caliban. Note that even Caliban has his own theology, which interested Browning. Prospero suggests that his greatest mistake was in teaching Caliban language, though we can scarcely regret it since some of the best lines are his. The sentimentalist will think that Prospero was not always discreet in his treatment of the brute-man: but whether by Setebos or Sycorax or the magician's harsh discipline, Caliban had been pretty well Nazified, even to the coincidence of a passion for book-burning. One of the problems that any kind of executive has to consider is how far to let his public into the secret of what he is doing to them. In his original job in Milan, Duke Prospero paid no attention to his public and got heaved out. Evidently the twelve years on the island have put new ideas in his head. He is wise enough, however, to put Miranda to sleep while he gives Ariel his instructions. But he wishes her to be sharply aware of Caliban and his dangers.

Even more than most of our collaborator's work, *The Tempest* is rich in double-talk. But in the passage of time some of his duplicities have lost their suggestion; consequently it is the more desirable to replace them with doublings of our own. Before dispersing his Ariel or secret mind to the elements he was setting down a kind of intellectual income tax report. His intellectual revenue, his depreciation and expense of spirit, are honorably noted, and he makes payment in his vision for humanity. Most scholars "discard" the sad little epilogue; the real epilogue is the greatest single speech in Shakespeare (Act IV, sc.i) "Our revels now are ended, &c."—I like to remember that the wisest of recent critics (Saintsbury) called it "perhaps the grandest example of the Grand Style in all literature." It is the one passage in Shakespeare that might have been expressly written for another magical island—Manhattan.

CONFLICT ON THE ISLAND

Prospero has escaped from the rivalries and cruelties of society into the selfish island of his own identity. It was his brother (Antonio) who desired to be "absolute" (as we would now say, "totalitarian"). It is silly to suppose that Shakespeare was just naïf in so frequently using the theme of struggle, rivalry, hatred, between brothers. Shakespeare was nobody's fool and I believe he wished to suggest by his fratriphobias the savage bitterness of every civil war between two opposing phases of the same idea. The same quality of concentration which Prospero put upon his studies appeared in Antonio as the passion for political power. Antonio says of himself that his spirits are nimble; it is he who tries to needle the lethargic Sebastian.

Even in the island of his inward exile Prospero finds again the elements of conflict. On one hand, the lovely and innocent Miranda whom the spectator may fabulize according to his own need. Philip Barry would call her Liberty Jones. She is actually the first white American girl in literature—about the same date as the real Virginia Dare (who, I learn in the Columbia Encyclopaedia, was the daughter of Ananias Dare). Bermuda was discovered in 1609 by Somers; if Shakespeare thought of Miranda as then fifteen, she was born about 1594. Virginia Dare was born in 1587 at Roanoke; but we have only the testimony of Ananias. Perhaps Virginia Dare and Miranda Prospero were the same? Sometimes one likes to think of her as the unspoiled possibility of American democracy, call her Columbia the Gem of the Ocean. Or you may metagrobolize her as the plastic elements of youth anywhere and any time.

Over against this attractive child stands the three-generation adversary Setebos-Sycorax-Caliban. One does not take the Caliban family with too professorial seriousness but our collaborator evidently means some suggestion of a principle of evil: beginning as mercurial intellectual evil (note the sharp snakelike hissing syllables of *Setebos* and *Sycorax*) and draining or loosening down to the big, clumsy, heavy-footed carnality of Caliban, in whom, however, are the yeasting convulsions of raw sensibility. Our collaborator has too much sense to think all this "out." Simply he *feels* it, as he intends us to do.

The trio Prospero-Miranda-Ariel are in command, in opposition to Setebos-Sycorax-Caliban, until the accident of the storm—note that it occurs during a fascist attempt to take over the African coastline; most magnificent 1941 coincidence. The shipload of symbolical fascists lands at the Bermuda soul base. (There are plenty of naval bases in the Caribbean but Prospero's island is the great intellectual base, which Shakespeare now offers to us on a lease-lend agreement if we know how to use it.)

The Tempest is perhaps both the subtlest and the simplest political and spiritual fairytale in our language. As Prospero says, his project "gathers to a head"—the head of the spectator. While it moves, "Times goes upright with his carriage." Of all contemporary writers perhaps Aldous Huxley has been most alert to Prospero's provocations and Miranda's phrase "Brave New World." On this island-base of western freedom, Caliban-Mussolini and Sycorax-Hitler come to shipwreck and it is even a shipwreck such as described by our magician which has in it no hatred for the unlucky millions behind these adventurers. Even they had their vision of a different world; but the new order cannot turn from west to east. Our collaborator in this last desperate testament was looking west for the first time.

"VANISHES IN THUNDER"

"He vanishes in thunder——" I can't read the words or say them without thinking of Hitler. I have tried not to give too much importance to the fables I find for myself in Shakespeare's fancy. Is it fair to dope a great innocent work of art with the drugs and poisons of our momentary need? Then I reflect that one quality of art is complete volatility in time. Never forget that Prospero's island is inside the reader's head; time can never penetrate the skull.

I had always thought that the horseplay of Trinculo creeping under Caliban's "gaberdine" was sorry groundling stuff; but revise Caliban and Trinculo as Hitler and Mussolini and see what a gorgeous cartoon. Consider Stephano's comment on this axis: "His forward voice is to speak well of his friend; his backward voice is to utter foul speeches." Most of Europe has crept under Caliban's blanket, and it has indeed a fishy smell.

The epitaph for most Shakespeare commentators is the stage direction for the Reapers in the masque: "To a strange, hollow, and confused noise, they Heavily Vanish." So I'll hand the script to some unspoiled producer—maybe even William Saroyan, who has the right initials—and do just that.

You cannot live forever on that Island. It fades like the smoke ring from Prospero's cigarette which opens my version. It is buried many fathoms more than five. Let the customer think of it as he will. He can conjecture the blue-eyed hag Sycorax as Aryan or Nordic bigotry. Ariel's pipe and tabor may be a memory of the tropical insect-noises that scared the voyagers at night. Prospero he can speculate as Science, or Democracy, or Uncle Sam, or Thought itself. Or he can let the words drift away above him like sky-writing in April. The point is that after borrowing bolus-plots all his life, our collaborator suddenly took his own mind for script. Thus he is "anchored in the bay where all men ride."

Bacon's Essays[1]

CHANCE HAS IT THAT THE TABLE WHERE I WRITE THIS IS COV-
ered by a sheet of glass. Through my sleeves I feel the chill of
that cold slippery stuff. How I would prefer to dictate, for
none can match written words with Lord Bacon. Only the
humble working impromptu of live speech could stand up to
that dark angel of English prose. It would be less wary than
this, but more manly. Yet I feel, or have persuaded myself, that
this cold plate under my elbows is somehow appropriate.

There is chill in the Essays too. It runs up the arms, it leaves
one a little sick and shaken. Perhaps nowhere in literature do
we more clearly see a Mind at work, and it frightens us. My
Lord's Northern Lights burn and steam like dry ice; our reason
is thrilled, but also (in his own words) we find we are 'full of
melancholy and indisposition, and unpleasing to ourselves.' It
is indeed 'a medicine too piercing and corrosive.' We have

[1]Copyright, 1944, by The Limited Editions Club, Inc.

passed winter evenings with him: he had the closer ingle of the hearth, wore his furred gown, sat (I suppose) on a woolsack, firelight shone through his wineglass and his thin clerkly hands. (Little else ever slipped between his fingers.) We were catching cold but we listened to his icicle aphorisms as he bent toward the fire and talked over his shoulder. 'Rising to great place is by a winding stair,' he remarked. He suggested 'the regulating of prices of things vendible,' and added that after a war the soldiers will require 'donatives.' If we grew restless he said 'stay a little that we may make an end the sooner.' He quoted Solomon: 'Prudens advertit ad gressos suos,' and was pleased by our version, 'The wise man watches his step.' He must have heard us sneeze, for he muttered 'qui fortiter emungit, elicit sanguinem.' We tried, bashfully, to express astonishment at the frostfires of beauty that coruscate—even against his will—in the arch of his arctic sky. 'Beauty,' he mused, 'hath ever some strangeness in the proportion. It comes by a kind of felicity, and not by rule.—But enough of these toys.'

There have been some, who had winter-talk by the fireside, or aestivated with him in that great plotted garden (what a man he was for blueprints) and came away whispering, 'The old son-of-a-bitch.' That also can be true. He's like iced vermouth; lucid and orderly as a telephone book. 'The great snake,' Lytton Strachey called him in a memorable and excited passage. My Lord's retort probably was that Strachey was 'infected with the style of the poets, speaking in a perpetual hyperbole.' Others remember the smell of the mint-beds in the garden, and the wizened old chancellor treading them with his heel. So he trod out the savors of language. His abrupt felicities were all the more startling from so bony a mind. There was mustard as well as mint in that garden. He liked the mustard-seed: 'it hath a property and spirit to get up and spread.' Often he forgot our frailty and would soliloquize in Latin, old master of a double tongue. 'Qui mari potitur, eum rerum potiri,' he said (I think he was quoting Tully; or Mahan?). It was well in character that when planning his imagined country seat he specially approved bay windows—not for their view of landscape, but because they are good retiring places for conference. He was always in conference with himself.

So he usually sent us away early. 'He that is too much in anything, so that he giveth occasion of satiety, maketh himself cheap.' We always hoped to get an autograph letter from him, but he said, 'It is better to deal by speech than by letter. Letters are good when a man would draw an answer by letter back again.' He paced a whole length of the mustard and watercress beds and then added, 'Or when it may serve for a man's justification afterwards to produce his own letter.'

Someone said he had seen few women of quality about the estate at St. Albans. They did not seem amused by My Lord. Probably he said once too often, 'These are but toys.' It was odd that the notion of Bacon having written Shakespeare began (or anyhow was strongly forwarded) among females. Sensitized to poets, one might expect a bluestocking to think that two more diverse minds never lived. Yet I'm not so sure. Lovers of thought have a good instinct that the essence of mind is everywhere the same. Bacon wrote his Essays young, as Shakespeare his Sonnets. The moods were completely different, but I suspect there were as many erasures when Bacon tried to say how clearly he thought as when Shakespeare tried to say how confused he felt. We are told that the Essays were revised in the last year of Bacon's life, brought down to date, after his political downfall, either as apology or as defiance. (I prefer to think the latter.) Of course no one revises sonnets. One might as well try to revise an influenza.

It would be happy—the easy happiness of scholars—to go on repeating how different were Bacon and his everlasting rival. But I don't know. I open the book almost at random, where he is dealing not with social stratagem but with doom at large. Erase a syllable here and there, reset as verse, and what have you:—

> But I consent with Caesar, that the sudden
> Passage is easiest; and nothing more
> Awakes resolve and readiness to die
> Than quiet conscience, strengthened with opinion
> That we shall be well spoken-of on earth
> By the just, and by the family of virtue.
> The opposite is fury to a man,
> Makes even life unsweet. What is more heavy
> Than evil fame deserved . . . he that, yet living,
> Follows the funerals of his reputation.

Would you know, old mole, who wrote it? It's from the fragment on Death, a topic even Bacon thought important enough to treat twice. To use his favorite metaphor, when great minds deal with the same theme they have their individual orbits, but are also quietly carried by the Primum Mobile. Frostbitten or not, in the Essays you will find as much of mind's Prime Movers as in anything written to the same purpose, to disregard ecstasy and convey judgement.

Like the atheism he spoke of, wisdom (even his) was more on the lip than in the heart. I wonder how he may have readjusted the Essays (to serve as mutes in the funeral of his reputation) when he revised in 1625. I suppose the existing copies (only seven, I believe) of the 1597 edition have been collated with the later volume, and experts must have noted how he rewrote.

Even for a writer of prefaces, the Essays are great preachers of brevity. His 'plausible' (viz., praiseworthy) gnomes have been copiously corroborated in all history since. In his piece on Dissimulation is a passage that might have been written as a memo for Franklin Roosevelt in 1944. You will read, I hope, not methodically but dipping here and there, sometimes pausing for the digestive chew he advised. You will find character in the fact that he is at his incomparable best on painful or executive themes—for instance, Revenge, Dissimulation, Envy, Studies, Sedition, Cunning, Dispatch, Negotiating, Vain-Glory, Anger. Whatever you do, don't miss him on Travel. But in whatever mood, he can render as acid intellectual pleasure as print affords, and always the felicity of Lucifer. One would not praise too glibly: he pointed out, the praise of the ignorant is worth nothing.

As I write this it is snowing; one remembers the legend that a spring snowstorm killed him. He died as he lived, in a practical zeal for exact knowledge. To learn whether refrigeration really arrests decay he went outdoors to buy a drawn fowl and stuff it with snow. Maybe the Essays have kept so well, and will keep forever, for that same reason. Their entrails are packed with ice.

(Feb. 29, 1944)

The Sense of Place[1]

ENGLAND IS A LAND THAT MADE FRIENDS WITH HERSELF; WITH
her natural genius. Her political puberty began early. Prodigious biological shuffling, a climate that encouraged indoor
meditation, and a landscape bewitched with bashful beauty—
variously beautiful, but never spectacular—begot quicksilver
fancy upon a carnal and sombre people. In that island of disillu-
sioned and temperate humor, man has most continuously and
eloquently recorded the mortal effort to rise above our own carcass—and still enjoy the carcass. "There'll always be an England" was one of the casual gnomes of this era, and that same
England will always be to other nations a special paradox: at
once a museum piece of ancient magic and the most diligently
foresighted of modern democracies. Both Dr. Goebbels and the
Chicago *Tribune* have frequently intoned a Litany for Britain;
the only response has been grim cockney laughter.

[1]Copyright, 1944, by Time, Inc.

There was a sign I used to see years ago on many pubs along the eastern docksides of London River. It said COURAGE'S STOUT. It was tragically prophetic; but also symbol and summary.

The best substitute for eternity is perfect suggestion of the momentary. The mind is freakish in choosing the moment it would perpetuate. In a London paper (in 1930) among advertisements of Landed Estates I saw that the Earl of Verulam was offering for sale his great property at St. Albans, "including the historic ruins of Bacon's house . . . completely walled kitchen gardens . . . valuable watercress beds." Then to me that estate became real: lo, here the actual gardens where the first Verulam plotted his alleys of thyme and mint and cress. Now I see him forever pacing an appetizer on his sunset path, scheming simultaneously in English and Latin while he bruises the mint beds with his heel— "to have the pleasure when you walk or tread." Since first reading that scented passage even my Lord's meanest stratagem acquires a peppermint flavor.

Or I see Hazlitt—but we better let him see for himself. No one of our tongue has had keener sense of Place:

> . . . one day after a sultry walk in summer between Farn-ham and Alton. I was fairly tired out; I walked into an inn-yard (I think at the latter place). The room I entered opened into an old-fashioned garden, embellished with beds of larkspur and a leaden Mercury; it was wainscoted, and there was a grave-looking, dark-coloured portrait of Charles II hanging over the tiled chimney-piece. I had Love for Love in my pocket, and began to read; coffee was brought in a silver coffee-pot; the cream, the bread

and butter, everything was excellent, and the flavour of
Congreve's style prevailed over all.[2]

These are mental pictures only, revived in selfish enjoyment.
How much more mystery, and a deep riddling pleasure, in the
photographer's image of any scene, whether familiar or strange.
We con it over, examine the accidents of light and pose. We
enjoy for an instant that exquisite fix, Fitz-Omar's "moment's
halt, the momentary taste of being." We are granted, in the eye
and the anxious mind, what we so fondly suppose we desire:
permanence. Then to that wish for seeing steadily and whole is
joined the pleasure of great words in alliance. It is a moment of
pure feeling and complicated joy. We are in a mood to relish
such wise dreamers as George Santayana:

> The human mind at best is a sort of song; the music of
> it runs away with the words, and even the words, which
> pass for the names of things, are but poor wild symbols
> for their unfathomed objects.[3]

The best prologue to this album of symbols would be in
verse. It would be, if honest, reminiscent verse; when I was a
boy on a bicycle exploring England, more than thirty years
ago, I wrote among earnest notes of ambition a memo that a
wonderful textbook of English literature could be made with

[2] I can't help thinking that Hazlitt, like all essayists who live in the
mind and not in memoranda, may have got his direction reversed? The
Bush Hotel at Farnham, which James Bone took me to see in 1947, still
looks much as Hazlitt described; the panelled coffee room is still named
for Charles *First;* there is the old-fashioned garden, and the unique sundial *on the ceiling,* which reflects the hours indoors by a mirror. That
Hazlitt did not notice, but all his friends tell us how his gaze was always
broodily downward. "Shoe-contemplating," I think Lamb said.

[3] In the prologue of his *Soliloquies in England* (1922), a book of the
rarest sensibility and surmise. He also treads on mint.

bicycle and kodak. I was always a great map-reader, and one of the astonishments of England to an American boy was how you could study one of Bartholomew's glorious survey-sheets at random and always come upon some place-name that started induced resonance. It usually happened after you had left the neighborhood of what you might have wished to see. But still to spy over the green and pink and brown of Bartholomew's elevations, enlarging detail with a reading lens, brings landscape alive. It is like being in a plane—like being a skylark—hills, hedgerows and villages are spread in depth beneath you, and a name that was only an allusion is suddenly a Place. The Shakespeare Cliff or the stripling Thames, Sherwood Forest or Malvern Hills, Runnymede or Merrow Down, these are not just "literature," they are human lives and thoughts. To me the best Basic English is always the map.

So I think with gratitude of the two young men who were ardent enough, in a difficult time, to study the map to such good purpose. As Donne exclaimed: "Pictures in their eyes to get, was all their propagation." The pictures they chose may be different from some yourself might have taken; that is of course, for the field is endless. Their pilgrimage was, in the English phrase that used sometimes to annoy us, "an American kind of thing to do." It was enormously worth doing if it reminds the mere verbalist that even the most far-travelled fancies had circumstance and local habitation.

Men's lingering thoughts can put strangeness upon the actual; place and feeling make the mutual courtesy of art. The picture herein of the two swans reminds me of a summer dusk when a friend and I loitered by the old stone bridge at Henley on the Thames. Four swans were coming downstream; they spread apart, apparently in practised calculation, and slid with cotillion

timing each through one of the four low arches—like four lines
of a perfect quatrain. Not Shakespeare nor Shenstone could
have patterned it better. Sometimes it seems that even earth and
creatures have been unlawfully aware. You can quote climate
and geography and food and fog and still not explain it all.
Unless you are foreign, of course you will never struggle to
explain it; but to a visitor the comedy and the queerness will
always occur. So it is Conrad the Pole, or James Bone and
Macdonell, Scotsmen, or Brogan, Scotch-Erse, or Capek the
Czech, or Santayana the don who is really a Don, who bespeak
England best in recent prose, so far as prose can measure. What
the Royal Navy calls the Western Approaches are more likely
to be baffled. What is the simple Yank to think of a nation
whose prime minister is so evidently part bulldog and part elf?
Is it not sensationally odd that one of the most perceiving (and
foreboding) tributes to British character was in Hitler's *Mein
Kampf?* The instant you begin to get heavily sentimental about
Britain she will grieve you by some sturdy sardonic rebuff. Be-
ware of supposing, from glimpses of antique renown, that she
is minded only toward the Past. No people in history has
thought harder of shapes to come.

The shabbiest sentimentality is to be ashamed of honest emotion toward things of noble memory. In the book of living are
many passages that were marked by pleased or startled readers;
the pages of England have been ticked in every margin by centuries of notation. Since we quoted Hazlitt's walk from Farnham to Alton (about ten miles), what else might he have seen
in that neighborhood? Let's get out the map of Surrey (with a
little bit of Hampshire) and have a look. If he had gone in the
other direction, toward Guildford, he might have made a de-

tour past Waverley Abbey, for which Scott's novels were named; and Moor Park, where Swift met Stella. Or, on the road to Alton, the first fork to the left would have brought him to White's Selborne, and Woolmer Pond where "some young men went down to hunt flappers." (This amused the boys of my generation; but flappers meant wild duck.) A few minutes' walk beyond Alton and he could have had his coffee—or tea, more likely—with Jane Austen. The same length of walk to the north would have reached Eversley, where a future rector would write *The Water Babies* and *Westward Ho*. A few miles to the south, across the gorse of Hankley Common, was Hindhead where *The Hound of the Baskervilles* was getting ready to be written a hundred years later. If he had stayed in Farnham he could have had his coffee, eventually, in the house where Cobbett was born. All these social possibilities in a few square inches of map taken at random.

No wonder we look with bifocal eyes on our envoys' glimpses where time and space are merging traffic. Was it behind one of these windows that Keats wrote to Fanny Brawne about spilling the currant jelly on his friend's *Ben Jonson?* Will the Bile Beans (see Piccadilly Circus) really keep us Happy and Slim, and Wrigley's give us "Vigour"? And there's an awning marked "S & G for tobaccos"—Good old Salmon & Gluckstein! There if anywhere you might find a copy of Sherlock Holmes's monograph, *Upon the Distinction Between the Ashes of the Various Tobaccos*. On Wimpole Street we see by the sign that the Barretts lived only seven doors from the corner of Weymouth Street. Was it round that corner Robert Browning had the carriage waiting? There seems to be a car parked at the wrong "kerb." By the lie of the shadows we guess the camera was looking south and the picture taken in the forenoon. I study these pictures as if I had taken them myself for that imagined boyish textbook. I remember when I first thought of it, sitting on the graveyard wall at Edmonton, trying to do a pencil sketch of the church where Charles Lamb is buried. Like all healthy young men I was great on graveyards in those days: Stoke Poges, of course; and an easy bike ride from there was Jordans for William Penn, and Beaconsfield for Edmund Waller who girdled a woman's waist with the prettiest verses ever written. Or it might be Old Fitz near Woodbridge, with the Persian rose by the stone; or that tablet at Stanton Harcourt to the lovers killed by lightning while embraced in a haystack. Pope wrote their epitaph (he always approved couplets) but it was thought too sprightly.

Student pilgrimages were not all so obviously romantic. I was equally thrilled by a country railway platform in Suffolk where a meeting with a professor turned young Stevenson's ambition toward writing; or the brook at Ashbourne in Derbyshire where Bozzy found Dr. Johnson trying to pole the dead cat over the dam. "This may be laughed at," says Boswell, "as too trifling to record." But in the margins of literature nothing is trifling. My friend Mifflin and I had cycled to Ashbourne (in the unreplaceable year 1911) as much on Izaak Walton's trail as on Dr. Johnson's. Rolling in summer sunset into the limestone hills of the Peak, how surprised we were to find a signpost pointing "To Haddon Hall." Simple Philadelphians, we had thought that was only a hotel in Atlantic City. We even pushed our bikes up 1690 feet to the Cat and Fiddle, the loftiest pub in England. If these explorers some day give us a sequel (and I hope they will) I beg for a picture of Dove Dale, where Dr. Johnson found the scenery for his Happy Valley in *Rasselas*.

So one is tempted to jot down further imaginary visit and search. Lulworth Cove, on the coast of Dorset, where the *Maria Crowther* lay offshore and Keats saw the bright steadfast star of the Last Sonnet—Blake's cottage at Felpham where he conversed with Homer, Dante and Milton on the beach, even as Walt Whitman did at Coney Island—or the lovely old twi-gabled church at Dean Prior where Rev. Robert Herrick preached and then walked home for Sunday dinner with Prew, the maid, and Tracey, the spaniel. Or my own secret unaccomplished pilgrimage to the parishes I once spotted on the map of Norfolk: Great and Little Snoring. Imagine, to be vicar of Great Snoring. . . . I said once, "I'll never see those old places now," and a young woman replied with memorable enigma: "Don't worry, you always carry your own ruins with you."

I didn't mean to get so far off the beam, but this book sends the mind on curves. I was trying to think about the Sense of Place. Only from that humble footing, companionship with things of sight and touch, can the mind rise to larger vantage. The Place may be anywhere and happens by chance. The liveliness of what they now call Regional literatures in the U.S. shows the growth of that sense of actual surrounding. In my own case it happens that Tintagel means less to me than Hoboken; Riverside Drive is quite as thrilling as Plymouth Hoe, and some scrubby woods on Long Island as truly haunted as Windsor Forest. That must be privately so for all. Any place is dear where a human mind rose above the joy and torture of the flesh and said its triumphant word—

> When artists bend their dreams and hands
>   All ages with one key unlock,
> And Master Shakespeare's yellow sands
>   Are on the shores of Paumanok.

The Bird that
Didn't Go South[1]

"THE G. R. PIPILO TOWHEES, SOCIALLY PROMINENT" (SAID the newspaper column) "are coming north earlier than usual. Pipilo, or Pip as his intimates call him, left Olive at Winter Park while he looks round the fashionable North Shore for a summer bungalow. Olive Towhee, an attractive brunette, was, of course, a Finch, of Virginia: a distinguished musical family."

Mr. Mistletoe had noticed this in the paper (he gets a lot of amusement from the social notes) and when he heard all that rustling and scratching in the dry leaves round the Knothole— a cabin in the woods of Long Island—he knew who it was. Towhee's first initials stand for Ground Robin, which many people call him; but he isn't a robin at all, in spite of the handsome ruddy lapels on his vest. His scientific nickname, Pipilo, simply means chirper, from the Latin verb *pipilare*, to chirp. He is a cheerful, friendly creature, short and plump but erect

[1]Copyright, 1939, by The United Newspapers Magazine Corporation.

221

of carriage. In his black tail coat and white vest he looks rather like a banker or economic royalist passing the plate in church. He likes to say that he keeps his feet on the ground, and, in fact, he spends most of his time rummaging rather noisily among thickets.

He and Mrs. Towhee build their home low, among dead leaves and twigs, and the family sometimes gets walked on.

Mr. Mistletoe came to the conclusion last spring that Pipilo is rather a stupid fellow. One day Pip saw his reflection in a side window of the garage. That window is in shadow and makes a perfect mirror. It was at the height of the sentimental season, and Pipilo at once supposed that Olive had come north to join him, and someone had shut her up in the garage. Day after day he spent hours on the sill, coaxing and serenading his own image until his throat was hoarse, and struggling to push through the pane.

There was a kind of pathos in this futile devotion. All the Mistletoes tried to disillusion him; repeatedly shooed him away. But he kept it up for weeks—until, I suppose, the genuine Mrs. Towhee arrived and took him in charge. Then they were busy raising a family somewhere in the wood lot, and like all conscientious husbands he sank out of sight.

Mr. Mistletoe forgot about him until autumn. Most of the birds went south rather early that year: I think perhaps they had private warning of the big September hurricane. But Pipilo, obstinate as usual, delayed his departure. Evidently he came through the great windstorm all right, but it must have given him a scare. One afternoon about the end of September Mr. Mistletoe found him inside the garage, fluttering angrily against a window pane at the back.

Housewives would have said it was so long since Mr. Mistletoe had cleaned those windows they couldn't have fooled any-body; but they deceived Pipilo. Instead of flying out through the wide-open double doors, he kept battering against the glass.

Mr. Mistletoe attempted with tactful gestures to wave him in the other direction, but Pipilo only became more frantic with perplexity. Finally, fearing the socially prominent creature would hurt himself, Mr. Mistletoe grabbed him as he stood baffled on the sill. He carried him toward the open doorway. But just as they got there Pipilo gave a convulsive jerk. He wriggled himself free and shot off—leaving half his tail feathers in Mr. Mistletoe's hand.

Mr. Mistletoe, meditating (for the thousandth time) that it's probably better not to interfere in other people's problems, saw with anxiety that Pipilo could no longer fly straight. He started off in a beeline toward Florida, but he kept taking a slew to the right and trying to correct it. He nearly collided with the corner of the house, but got past it and then climbed for eleva-tion. The last we saw of him he was traveling fast but making a lot of leeway. Mr. Mistletoe felt badly about this, and stuck the little sheaf of feathers in a crack in the garage door as a remembrance.

The fashionable bird colony at Winter Park waited in vain that year for the arrival of one of its most popular members. But if you suppose this is a sad story you are mistaken. Quite a while later Mr. Mistletoe learned what had happened: Towhees are not long-distance aviators; they are heavy eaters and their wings are small. They fly low and fast but with great exertion, and their long tails are important for balance. Pipilo, impulsive and determined as always, set off for Florida, but didn't realize how much drift and sideslip he was making.

Instead of following the usual straight line down the coast

(first stop somewhere near Barnegat) he kept wabbling west-ward. He tried to rectify this bad steering by using his right wing much harder than the left, and soon became exhausted. Somewhere near Newark, New Jersey, about sunset, he saw wide open fields and many enormous birds coming to earth. He followed their example and came downward. He coasted, braked a little with the underside of his wings, and expected to make a perfect landing.

But, due to fatigue and his accident, he muffed it. He found himself nose-heavy and dived too steep. Then, when he lifted his tail plane to retard the drop, he forgot that one whole side of his tail was missing. He banked sharply, lost his fore-and-aft trim, did a tailslip, and pancaked. He came down with a bump on hard concrete and lay in a faint, right in front of the Air-ways Building at the Newark Airport.

A big passenger plane had just come in from the west and the stewardess was leaving with her neat little bag of chewing gum and her first-aid kit. She picked up Pipilo, carried him to the rest room and gave him what they call Personalized Service. The pilots, who notice everything, had not missed this episode.

"Did you see that bird?" said one. "To my way of thinking he didn't act according to Hoyle."

"He must have lifted his elevator too quick."

"And he dropped his starboard aileron."

"Of course he yawed over and started to roll."

"Sure, the starboard wing had less lift."

"Then he tried to correct the aileron drag, and stalled him-self."

"He don't know his aerodynamics."

"Maybe something wrong with his rudder."

224

"Let's go see."

It was a good excuse to have a parting word with the pretty stewardess. Of course, when they saw that the right half of Pipilo's tail was missing, they understood perfectly and were professionally sympathetic. "It reminds me," said one, "of that time we tore off the fin going over a church steeple in a fog."

"He's got to get that tail plane fixed," one agreed, "or he'll be grounded for good."

Airplane stewardesses are ingenious; they like to call themselves Jills of All Trades. This one happened to have in her off-duty hat a smart little fan of feathers nearly the right size. (You can find almost anything in ladies' hats.) These, trimmed with nail scissors and fastened with a drop of liquid cement, made a very fine substitute tail.

Pipilo was too tired, and too groggy from a drop of brandy they gave him, to protest. But when they encouraged him to fly with his new equipment he showed no desire to do so.

I think he felt that the cement wasn't very secure and didn't wish to take chances. It's a long way to Florida, and he knew when he'd had enough.

"Let's take him on for a mascot," said one pilot.

"We'll have to get permission from the department," said the other. "You know the rules: no passengers in the control cabin."

It took some formality to get the license, but finally the Department of Commerce came through. Now Pipilo rides regularly between Newark and Chicago. He is perfectly content, perched in a cage above the pilots—indeed he's as good as a gyroscope. He has no ambition to fly under his own power (he's getting stout), but he knows all the theory by instinct.

Automatically he adjusts himself to the proper angles and air-flow pressures, and his behavior during a difficult maneuver has often given valuable suggestions to the pilots.

Perhaps Pipilo wasn't really so stupid after all.

The Consolable Widow[1]

THE GIST OF IT IS THIS: UNDER WHAT CIRCUMSTANCES WOULD a lawyer leave his briefcase behind after calling on a lady client?

Perhaps it's a story for professional men only, for whom a briefcase is almost a limb. The affair Had Everything (except a solution). There were picturesque setting, wild autumn rainstorm to wash blood and footprints, wagonwheels and voices heard in the night, and watchdogs that strangely were not heard. And behind the bizarre and brutal details was the somewhat multiple sex-appeal of a Consolable Widow. Even, if we listen closely, an overtone of literary art, for when one of Connie's letters was read aloud in court it caused in the audience "a murmur of charm and surprise." I'm afraid it loses in translation:

"Now almost three months without seeing you, without hearing the sound of your voice. Three months? Don't they seem

[1]Copyright, 1946, by The American Mercury, Inc.

more like three years? Not those former monotone years when I had no thoughts at all, but years full of uncertainty and anguish. Oh absence! Impatience for the return of the well-beloved! To think that one might have him with one, on one's lips, in one's arms, against one's heart—and be telling him I love him in a hundred thousand ways."

It loses also by the fact that Connie (short for Consolable) copied into an account-book the best love letters, both Incoming and Outgoing. Effective passages were used more than once. These were the only accounts she kept with any care.

Enough of prologue. I should add only that two recent reprints of an old story about the Bad Girl and the Bailiff, viz. the murder of Gouffé,[2] have brought comment which encouraged this *encore*. The present resurrection, also drawn from Bataille, is in a higher social bracket but in some sense a sequel.

I haven't been there, but it sounds like good country. Chantelle, a village of 1300 people, is in the valley of a stream deliciously named the Bouble. The hills slope up toward the great *massif* of Auvergne; there are vineyards to catch the sun, and a little narrow-gauge railway that joins the main P.L.M. line below Moulins. A Blue Guide of 20 years ago credits the toy train with a schedule of 48 miles in 5 hours, but I'm sure it compensates by the pitch and frequency of its shrill whistle. The engine frightens up puffs of white butterflies in the fields, and carries a jack on its bumper in case of trouble. The little

[2]See *The Red and White Girdle* (1931) reprinted by Louis Greenfield in an omnibus volume *Variety* (1944), and by Joseph Henry Jackson in *The Portable Murder Book* (1945). Those who might be interested in Albert Bataille's wonderful series of annual volumes, *Causes Criminelles et Mondaines,* probably the best crime reporting of its kind, will find him further exploited in my *Off the Deep End* (1928) and *Internal Revenue* (1933).—C.M.

station and freight-shed smell of wine-drippings, for the flat-cars are loaded with casks; nothing *tête de cuvée*, probably, but a modest Beaujolais; a bright ruby color with a strawberry taste, sometimes not even bottled but drunk straight from the wood.

Visitors to Chantelle would stop at the modest Hôtel de la Poste to take a glass of the local *cru* and forget their troubles a while. The sun is running its westing down, behind the peaks of the Puy de Dôme; the ruins of the Bourbon castle command the shallow valley. Then they see (I assume it's still there) a smart little villa on the uphill street. It has green blinds, and a tile roof with pigeons. A large walled garden actually includes some of the Bourbon foundations, here overgrown into mounds and rockeries. There is a comic summerhouse like a Chinese pagoda, sandy paths among rose-beds, a lawn, an orchard, a greenhouse and a dove-cot. The mossy wall is 9 feet high and topped with broken bottles; it borders a cobbled alley that leads to a vigneron's wine-press, and there's a neat green door in the wall. And it is that garden door which we softly open—to Sunday evening, October 5, 1890.

One wouldn't expect to be doing legal business in a country village on Sunday evening, but M. Lépine was really troubled. His very special client Mme. Achet (whom we have nicknamed Connie; Bataille never tells us her first name) has got her affairs in a mess. So much so that she prefers him to call in the evening, to avoid publicity. I spoke of M. Lépine as a lawyer, but he wasn't quite that: he was the village *notaire*, for which we have no exact counterpart. The French notary (an officer of the state) seems to be a combination of accountant, trustee, legal counsellor and business agent; more like what is called in England a solicitor, or the Scots "Writer to the Signet." At any rate he has long handled the affairs of the gay little widow. Now they seem to approach a crisis. While M. Lépine is considering which of a number of papers to put in his briefcase for this Sunday evening call, we can catch up with some of the background that he knows by heart.

Mme. Achet, now age 32, was born to the excellent name of Prévost, daughter of a well-to-do business man in Paris. At 19 she was given to a husband 20 years her senior; one of those wedlocks that justified the cynical French saying "*Il-y-a de mariages agréables; il n'y en a point de délicieux*." M. Achet had a thrifty tutoring establishment in the neighborhood of the Sorbonne, where he coached backward boys for college entrance. We can speculate about that, but it would be only guesswork. At any rate the bride brought with her a handsome dowry, the ambitious don had saved some francs of his own, and three years after marriage they settled in the coquettish villa at Chantelle—perhaps because Mme. Achet's younger sister had married the druggist there, M. Demotte. Bataille says M. Achet was fed up with chewing Latin grammar. But he now began studying more dangerous declensions, those of the stock market. He was an imprudent investor, and when he died in 1885 he left his inexperienced wife with two children, a costly ménage, and an embarrassed estate.

But the young widow was by no means inclined to retrench. The notary Lépine, a man of her husband's age, had charge of her business; let him do the worrying. She had expectations from an uncle; and more tangible help from other sources. We must be a little more delicate than Bataille in our commentary, but after the monotone years with the tutor Connie began to sparkle. Perhaps there was a pathos in this frolic, for the older of her two children, a little girl, had died lately. At any rate she was living beyond any visible means of support, even making occasional trips to Paris. The narrow-minded little train trundled her down the valley of the Bouble, and perhaps there was censure in its shrill scream as she got aboard the main line at Varennes. The rest of the way was on broader gauge. She even kept a room—what is so inaccurately called a *pied-à-terre*—in the Boulevard de Strasbourg; certainly not a fashionable neighborhood, but convenient for her friend M. Delorme, the cashier of the Bee (Abeille) Insurance. He was a sturdy and reliable fellow with a spreading chestnut moustache; it must have been her idea, not his, that their correspondences were signed *Vivien* and *Ninette*. Delorme's tropes of sentiment probably followed the obvious suggestion of bees and honey.

Cashier Delorme was only one of Connie's invisible assets. The fiscal-minded Lépine, if he had known all details, might have said she liked to pyramid her transactions. To some of her friends the court granted a benignant anonymity: for instance Dr. X——, to whom "she gave herself in his clinic"; another we hear of only as one of those myriad mysterious Frenchmen called functionaries. Inescapably important was young M. Albert Thaunié, several years younger than herself, and rich, and not far away. He lived at the Château de Blanzat, where "he threw money out of the windows," he was expert with horses and dogs and sports, and spent much time hunting in the wilds of the Cévennes, where R. L. Stevenson only a few years before had travelled so harmlessly with a donkey.

But we must get back to the papers in M. Lépine's briefcase, which dealt with less romantic matter. There was the mortgage on the property which he had arranged for Mme. Achet. There were notes of the various advances he had made

to her from his own funds, mounting now to 10,000 francs—
over $2000, a lot of money. There were memos about the se-
curities in her husband's estate, whose yield had now dropped
to about $600 a year.

There had been a good deal of talk among the village *four-
nisseurs*, for Connie still lived high; old Françoise, the maid
(who was *"rien d'une soubrette"*), took in more game and fish
at that garden door than any other servant in town. Since
Lépine drew the dividends and paid the bills, there must have
been plenty of papers in the dossier. I see him spreading them
out under the lamp in his sitting room that Sunday evening,
deciding which it would be worthwhile to lay before his irre-
sponsible client. A tiresome fellow, poor Lépine, associated
in Connie's mind with tedious budgetings. Not an attractive
figure: we happen to know that he weighed 240 pounds; and
worse, he had a goitre. What we don't know, and never can,
was whether he had been entirely sincere in his loans and re-
proaches. There is at least a possibility he might not have
been dismayed at Connie's deficit. The mortgage principal was
soon due; he might buy it up himself and take over that attractive property? But a French notary, an officer bonded to
the State, is more likely to commit carnal delict than fiscal.
He is more likely to attack his client's person than her purse.
In settlement of the account, why not take over Connie herself? Lépine visualizes her: nimble, brunette, appetizingly
plump; not exactly pretty, but *gamine, piquante, mine chif-
fonnée*. Once he had read one of Paul de Kock's amusing novels
about Parisian modistes: that was what she was like. Bataille,
who had an eye for such things, describes the impudent little
hat Connie wore at the trial. You couldn't translate it, any

more than translate the hat itself to another head. It was part of her:

> . . . *le chapeau tout mignon, fait d'un rien, de quelques plumes et d'un peu de tulle sur une forme lilliputienne.*

This particular wisp of headgear Lépine never saw; but he had seen plenty like it. He sighs a little—or is it a grunt?—and puts 7200 francs in bank notes into the briefcase, no one knows why. He says goodnight to Mme. Lépine and his law-student son, sets off down the dark street. Were the 7200 francs cash to be a set-off against the I.O.U. for 10,000 he was going to force her to sign? All we know is the extraordinary fact that when he returned he had left the briefcase at Connie's. He said he forgot it. Connie said he left it of his own free-will; but she added, later, the deathless remark: "There are things of which one does not speak too categorically."

I can't be too categorical either. I have to accept as fact what Bataille accepted; but since I'm not liable, as he was, to "process of diffamation," I can redouble his informative spades. It would help if we knew that this Sunday evening meeting took place because Connie's wealthy uncle M. Moreau (former deputy) had died October 4. But when did she learn that? By telegram on Saturday, or by post on Monday? And how seriously did Lépine take her assertion that Uncle Moreau was going to leave her a legacy? Actually, we learn later, the uncle didn't.

What we do know is that when Lépine retrieved the brief-case it contained neither the 7200 francs nor the signed acknowledgment of his client's debt. I like to linger on the physical briefcase, one of those French portfolios, a foldover of well-worn leather and no handle, always hugged close to stout M.

Lépine's notarial breast. Briefcases have played a great part in my own life, I know how dear they can be; I have even used their scuffed and outworn hides for the binding of books. The briefcase is the professional man's breviary, his bourse, his book of common prayer. Connie said some astonishing things under question, which Bataille is too prudent to underline; one of them was "if you knew all about briefcases, you'd have the secret of many things."

My guess is that Françoise, the *bonne à tout faire*, carried the briefcase back to Lépine's office when she was sent to do the marketing on Monday. I think so because that same day (presumably while the *bonne* was out) the big carving knife disappeared from the kitchen dresser, and Françoise was puzzled.

Other things happened that day. Lépine made a note in his books "*Remis à Mme. Achet 7200 fr.*" If we knew just how to interpret *Remis* (it baffles Bataille too) it would help. Paid? Credited? Cancelled? Written off? And about the same time Connie was sitting in her little salon, opening onto the garden terrace, writing in that French purple ink on onionskin paper a letter to Cashier Delorme. He is to go to their little honeycomb on the Boulevard Strasbourg and get her revolver, have it repaired, and mail it to her. To M. Delorme's astonishment her letter enclosed a 1000 franc note, "for expenses."

Cashier Delorme knew (no one better) that his Queen Bee's fiscal methods were temperamental. He supposed she didn't want anyone in Chantelle to know she had so large a bill, and wanted it changed. Conscientious friend, he mailed her back ten 100-franc notes, but took his time about the revolver.

M. Lépine is also using pen and ink. Does he think he has paid too much for what he got, or didn't get? He is trying to recoup at least part of the 7200 francs. There is some to and fro about this, but the payoff is that Lépine says the matter must be settled by October 15. Is that some kind of quarter-day or statutory deadline in France? Anyhow Connie tells him to come to see her that day about 5 P.M.

A week goes by and Connie hasn't received the revolver. On October 13 she telegraphs M. Delorme the cryptic message: *Need silk by tomorrow.* Delorme guesses what she means, mails it at once, what we would now call parcel post special handling. He marks the parcel *Metallic Tubes;* an accurate-minded man.

In case, very unlikely, anyone should check me up, I must here mention discrepant data in Bataille. There were many queer inconsistencies in this case, and it seems that in his hasty memoranda Bataille got confused between 17,000 francs and the 17th of October. No one with a spider-web mind will be surprised by that. So I don't know, and it doesn't matter now, whether the crisis came on October 15 or October 17. The testimony gives both dates.

Whichever it was, at 5 P.M., as appointed, M. Lépine went to the *villa très coquette.* He rang at the front door, with its handsome iron grille. Mme. Achet sent word, by Françoise, that she was having a fitting with her dressmaker and couldn't see him. I imagine both indignation and fantasy in the mind of Lépine as he listens to Françoise at the door. "She can't see you now, she's all undressed, the couturière is running the tape around her." Whether as methodical notary or lickchop wooer, what could annoy him more? I myself am annoyed not to know what kind of costume was being measured, or fitted, or altered in haste. A little traveling *tailleur,* of warm tweed, suitable for a carriage drive late at night? Informed on this point, we might have a clue to Mme. Achet's plans for that evening.

It has been a bright autumn day; Connie was out in the garden that afternoon, cutting the late roses. But now, at dusk, it has turned windy, thickening for rain. There's a pleasant shine of lamplight from Françoise's kitchen, and a warm whiff of some *gibier* on the stove. Perhaps M. Lépine suggests he can wait a while, thinking he might be asked to share a dish of stew with his client. But hardfaced Françoise says, "She's going to dinner with her sister."

"Then I'll come back later," he says angrily.

Connie calls down from her bedroom—or so she insisted later —"You can't come tonight. I'm spending the evening with the Demottes" (her sister and brother-in-law). "I won't be back until late. Come tomorrow morning."

The dressmaker said nothing; her mouth was probably full of pins, and remained so, for her testimony, that might have been critical, does not seem ever to have been taken. But whether he made it plain to them or not, M. Lépine decided he would come back about 10 o'clock that night. He lumbered off, hugging his briefcase, down the village street, turning his collar against a sensation of chill. When he told his family he would have to go out again that evening and where, Madame Lépine was anxious. "I don't like it when you have to go to that house. I don't know why, I always think of Gouffé" (referring to the case that had made such a stir the year before).

The notary, his wife, and his law-student son played cards peacefully that evening. When he left the house, soon after ten o'clock, Madame Lépine had gone to bed, but she called out to him, "I think you ought to take your revolver." He did; but it may have been because the annual wine-harvest fair was to open the next day. There were rough characters in town, peddlers and itinerant pitchmen and grifters, and plenty of drinking in the little bistros. It was a black night now, and pouring rain; a wrong time for any mature businessman to be abroad, thought Mme. Lépine. But the notary insisted that his client was expecting him. He had to call on her so late because she did not wish anyone to guess how involved were her affairs.

Mme. Lépine was heartened by the fact that her husband left the lamp burning in his bedroom. Knowing his thrifty spirit, that must mean he wouldn't be gone long.

Mme. Achet, meanwhile, had been spending the evening as advertised, at the Demottes'. According to Adeline Demotte, her sister was in no hurry to leave, she wanted to continue the music they were enjoying, but the druggist was tired and wished his bed. When Françoise called for her, with the big umbrella, they pushed Connie out into the storm.

Through the cobbled streets, dimly glistening, we imagine those figures converging on the bijou villa. But from here we pass into a chapter of low visibility, as obscure as the night itself. The facts are few but horrid.

Françoise, probably muttering *"un sale temps,"* locked the front door, climbed to her room in the attic and heard nothing until morning. Connie was more leisurely. She undressed, made sure that the 7-year-old Ali (which I take to be a nickname, perhaps for Alexandre) was asleep in his room adjoining hers. Then she went into the little salon (on the same floor) which overlooked the garden terrace, "to put down her things" (*déposer mes effets*), when she heard a tapping at the window, and her name called. She opened without hesitation. It was M. Lépine.

"What on earth are you doing here?"

"I've come to settle my accounts," and he tried to force his way in. She says he threatened her with a revolver. Her own weapon, the "metallic tubes" mailed by Cashier Delorme, was lying on her desk. She ran for it, they wrestled together in the open window and fell onto the terrace. She fired her revolver, at random, and Lépine fled into the garden. She followed, shooting to hit. At the last shot he fell over a terrace, or a fragment of the old Bourbon wall, a drop of three meters.

She was in such a state (she says) that she ran madly round the garden thinking the villain might still pursue. But he lay still. Well he might; as M. Waldeck-Rousseau remarked later, she had made a bullseye on him five times out of six: in the spine, left shoulderblade, throat, right eye, and left lung. This marksmanship, to accept her own story, while running wildly through rain and dark.

She approached and found him dead. She returned to the house for her raincoat. She took the carving knife from the ledge of the pigeonhouse where it was conveniently lying (she had left it there after cutting roses that afternoon) and sliced the corpse's throat—a slash 20 centimeters long and 7 deep, right through the "voluminous goitre," as Bataille grue-somely insists. She removed his watch and papers, and carried (not dragged) the body (240 lbs.) fifty feet into the alley alongside the garden wall, where it lay under the sluice of a rainspout, draining and bleaching all night. She raked sand over the bloodstains, wiped her slippers with a napkin, washed the carving knife and put it back in the kitchen drawer. She concealed 7000 francs in bank notes in a fold of the hearth-rug. Then, in her own words, she threw the watch and papers down the watercloset, closed the window, and fell into bed. She had defended her honor, and slept sound until 9:30 A.M.

The purpose of these extraordinary maneuvers, she averred, was to suggest slaughter and robbery by prowlers of the night. This account, here so briefly summarized, she maintained unshaken during nine hours of questioning at the trial. Some of her answers were very brisk: for instance, as Holmes would have put it, the curious incident of the dogs in the nighttime. There were two dogs who usually slept on the terrace. Where were they that night, or why didn't they give alarm? Connie's reply: *"Il leur arrivait quelquefois de découcher"*—"sometimes they slept out."

But poor Mme. Lépine didn't sleep much that night. She kept waking, noticing always that the lamp in her husband's room was still burning. Finally, at dawn (which came clean, after the downpour), she sent her son to search, and herself went to the house of the priest for advice. Her thought, rather charmingly expressed, was that Mme. Achet had "sequestrated" her husband, in order to compel him to return home by daylight and cause a scandal. This is my evidence for thinking Mme. Lépine a good wife: she had loyally and unconsciously picked up her husband's semi-legal jargon.

It was worse than that. The wine-pressers were up at daylight, getting ready for a big day, and already, as young Emmanuel Lépine scouted the Achet villa, his father's body had been found in the alley. The young man came racing back in horror. "They've assassinated him!"

Now let's take up some of the questions that agonized not only Bataille, but two of France's greatest lawyers: M. Waldeck-Rousseau (afterward premier, and defender of De Lesseps in the great Panama Canal case two years later) and

M. Demange, eloquent champion of all kinds of female aberration. There is no ascertainable answer to some of these mortal uncertainties, but we have Posterity's only privilege: detached conjecture. We might even be fanciful and wonder if the trouble was partly due to season (the *vendange* or grape harvest) and climate (the bracing and mineral stingo of that upland air). Of Royat, only a few miles away, it was once said "the air would make a bishop bite a barmaid in the neck"; a casual remark that greatly increased Royat's tourist traffic. There are freaks and emanations in that region: at Royat, guide books tell me, there is the *Grotte du Chien* which exhales carbon dioxide enough to asphyxiate a dog, while a man, erect, feels nothing of it. Perhaps the dogs (*Nounou* and *Pioupiou* are my names for them) were stupefied by some noxious geological oxide. But I have my own theory about the dogs, which will appear.

Footprints. By the time the *juge d'instruction* (police magistrate) arrived from Gannat (legal headquarters of the district) all tracks in the garden had been erased, either by rain or carelessness. Here a side-issue of local politics became violent: Dr. Noir, the village physician for 25 years and its mayor for 15, was accused of having overtrodden a footprint that might have been important. This assertion was complicated by the fact that Dr. Noir was a Red Republican, and poor old Lépine was the local Tory, and was going to work against him in the coming elections.

Gendarmes. The village police seem to have been as futile as any in fiction. The constable set to watch the house did not notice when Mme. Achet sent young Ali with a parcel for Mme. Demotte, which contained her revolver; nor when

Connie's godmother, Mme. Desgranges of Paris, who mysteriously happened to be in Chantelle at the time (at the Demottes'?) took away a bundle of papers and money and a box of cartridges, confided to her by her godchild, and burned the papers. M. Lépine's office file was found to be empty of all documents in the Achet dossier.

Corpse. Was poor Lépine's throat cut while dead or still alive? Four doctors divided two to two on this. Could the body be *carried* (not dragged) by so small a woman as Connie? The police tried experiments on citizens of large stature hefted by women of Connie's size; inconclusive. The prosecution was outraged that Connie had never been "confronted" with the draggled blood-drained corpse; but there was plenty of it on the table of *pièces justificatives:* his stained enormous clothes; his revolver, found in the garden; and, bottled in alcohol, his "larynx," including the horrible carved goitre.

Bruises. Connie was shy about physical examination, which was odd, because it was the only confirmation of her story. She was found to have contusions on her arms, thighs, hocks (*jarrets*), shins, and right calf.

Throatcut. Again the doctors disagreed; could any woman have achieved, with one slash (as Connie insisted), such a wound in the throat? Her defence might have been, a widow has to learn to do the carving.

Garden Door. How could Lépine have entered unless the door in the wall, usually kept locked, was purposely left open? The jury was asked to consider three questions:

Was it a deliberate ambush, perhaps with an accomplice?

Was Connie defending her honor against an outrageous and unexpected assault?

Or did the notary's visit coincide malapropos with the arrival of an *expected* lover?

To these we should add two of Waldeck-Rousseau's shrewd inquiries: Can we blame the notary if he wanted a bite at the apple which so many had already tasted? And if she really picked up the body and carried it, why can't she describe how it was done?

Overheard. The child Ali (age 7), whose testimony was charitably taken not in open court but privately, under conditions of privilege, said he had been waked by hearing men's voices, indoors. Neighbor Martin, a carpenter, thought he heard shots but prudently stayed in bed. Widow Grandjean, "wrinkled like a winter apple," also heard what sounded like shots but told her beads again and pulled the quilt over her head. The tanner Auguste Melin, whose vats were nearby, got up during the night because he had some hides in pickle. He heard wagonwheels, hoarse voices, footsteps, and sounds of struggle. He heard the mysterious ejaculation *"Han!"* (as pronounced in French) and a cry *"Laissez-le là!"* He supposed that referred to a wagonload of grapes left near the neighboring wine-press. There were also bangs that might have been thumps on a door. How would you translate *"Laissez-le là"?* It might be Leave *it* there, it might be Leave *him* there. Melin did whatever a tanner does, and hurried back to bed. Who blames him?—he was in his nightshirt, no trousers on, and it was pelting rain. But his brother Antoine, a farmer, clouded the issue: he said that Auguste had told him he thought he recognized, in the shouts in the alley, one particular voice that rolled its r's (*grasseyait*) in the Auvergne accent. It was the miller Bouladon. And that brought out the strange fact that when the famous lawyers came to Moulins for the trial,

Bouladon had said, drinking at a pub, "The murder of Lépine? Shucks, I was there."

Special Train. This halted everything. The judge called a recess while they "heated up a special train" (*un train spécial est immédiatement chauffé pour aller chercher Bouladon à Chantelle.*) Can't you hear the narrow-gauge line whistling with excitement? Meanwhile I imagine Maître Demange and Maître Waldeck-Rousseau, taking a tiffin together at the Hôtel de la Poste, discussing with cheer and wit any other case but this; each privately thinking what surprises he has to spring on the other. Waldeck-Rousseau is remembering Connie's sprightly letters to various lovers: *par exemple,* to Dr. X—— of the unidentified clinic: "Let me come to you and be your little doctor in skirts." —And Maître Demange, never more *en verve* (says Bataille, who had listened to him often), is planning how best to introduce the fact that Connie had never taken Lépine seriously; she had called him, in English, a "fat goose."

Rolling R's. If you start picking at any knot in the great human snarl, you're sure to loosen strings into all sorts of trouble. Here's the poor little miller Bouladon, for whom the special train has been heated. Bataille says he looks "sad and poor, constrained and embarrassed, this has been for him a day of strong emotions." His testimony is pathetic. He admits he may have said something silly about the crime, to increase his importance. Ever since one of his children fell into the fire and was burned to death he has been a bit gaga, and after a drink or two he talks wildly. Moreover, the night of the tragedy he was at home: his wife was dying. The court keeps Bouladon talking so tanner Melin can estimate the roll of the r's. They are throaty enough, but now Melin isn't sure if that was the voice. No one seems to have remarked that in

243

the critical phrase overheard—*"Assez! assez! Laissez-le là!"*
there aren't any r's.

Dorothy Sayers, in one of her most brilliant books (*The
Mind of the Maker*, p. 188), has suggested that the human
passion for detective stories is due to the universal hankering
for "a final, complete, and sole possible solution." There is
nothing of that in this detective story without a detective.
It is a paradigm of perplexity; of the uncertainties of mortal
witness, especially when (like a conference of Foreign Minis-
ters) it has to be filtered by translation. How shall we estimate
Connie: by the impudent little hat, or by her attempt (locked
in jail at Gannat in a long cold winter) to commit suicide?
She hoarded lumps of coal sent for the stove in her cell; hid
them in her mattress, and tried to gas herself with them.—Or
do we estimate her by Honeyman Delorme's statement, that
when she asked him to send the revolver he was no more surprised than if she had asked for an umbrella?

No wonder I wish we still had William Bolitho to write
about these things; he understood, what Woollcott and
Roughead and Edmund Pearson never did, that crime is something more than a chance for the literary tipstaff to be jocular.
How do historians, so cool and vicious with postpositive wit,
sift their grains of judgment? The tanner Melin heard blows,
bangs, or thuds, and the cry *"Han!"* How do you interpret
"Han"? Larousse says it's the dull grunt of a man striking
a blow. The child Ali, half-awake—and is seven years an age
of verdict or of fantasy?—thinks he heard M. Lépine shout
"Holà! Holà!" What would you say about that? Look it up
in Larousse, or overhear it in a night of rain and murder?
Does it mean *Hullo, Hullo!* or *Stop, Stop!?* If you don't know
the timing and the tone of voice, you know nothing.

To simplify, I come back to the briefcase. I just don't believe that the notary forgot it. As Kipling said,

> Does the Maid forget both jewel and gem,
>   Or the Bride her wedding dress?
> Does the Jew forget Jerusalem,
>   Or the Printer forget the Press?

If Lépine left it behind it could only have been as part of what the French call a transactional formula. It was an earnest, a symbol, of favors already, he thought, overdue. It was a token of something not taken; an excuse to come again. When he did, with his fatal jest "I've come to collect," did he happen into another appointment? Connie was bored with bank balances and niggling notaries. She'd had thirteen years of tutoring long ago. Now she had her eye on something more solid, the Château Blanzat. Any moment now the wheels would grind up the cobbled alley; not a wagon of grapes but a more personal harvest. Why else the gun, the broken appointment, the dressmaker in haste, the careful alibi *chez Demotte?*

Bataille, always acute for drama, hates to let us down at the end. The jury, compromised by the rigor of Waldeck-Rousseau versus the wit of Demange, were out only 15 minutes. Connie was found guilty, with extenuating circumstances. "Still mysterious and impenetrable," she was sentenced to 12 years hard labor. That was May 3, 1891.

Not only hard labor, hard luck. The man who might have got her off (we know his chivalry for women in distress) was busy that weekend. The next day, Monday, while Connie was being hooted on the narrow gauge to the train for Montpellier Prison, Sherlock Holmes and Dr. Moriarty grappled at the Reichenbach Falls.

We know Holmes's special interest in Montpellier. He visited there during the famous absence 1891–94. He told Watson it was to do research in coal-tar derivatives, which led to oxides of uranium and you-know-what. Actually it was because he was curious about those two dogs in the nighttime. But he had a disappointment. In January 1892 Connie was declared insane and removed to an asylum. Bataille leaves her there, and I know nothing further. *Except*——

Consider the wolf-hunter.

M. Thaunié, the young aristocrat, had good reason to be grateful to Saint Hubert, patron of the chase. He had several witnesses to prove that on the fatal date he was in the woods and valleys of *la Creuse*, hunting wolves. But that's not far away (say, 40 miles), and sportsmen are notoriously generous in attesting each other. Bataille speaks guardedly about M. Thaunié. Although fifteen years younger than the ambrosial cashier, Bataille found the hunting squire the lesser fellow. (*"Beaucoup moins bien"*.) He had "an indecisive moustache" and was frightened on the stand. Had he advised Connie to take a revolver for their little trip? Well, not exactly; he had told her the roads weren't safe, and they would have to leave late at night to avoid comment.—When was this excursion to take place? That night?—Well, not precisely. The date hadn't been fixed; it was going to be a bit later.

Presumably there were wolves to be killed first. Was the notary one of them? Consider two possible points. There was mighty good shooting done on Lépine, which suggests an experienced marksman. Who but the wolf-hunter could do that accurate shooting? And of all people concerned, Thaunié was most familiar with dogs. Was that why they didn't bark? They knew him already? They were from his own hunting kennel at Château de Blanzat, and he had given them to her? Even perhaps a third point: several people testified to hearing wheels in the night. They were thought to be the wagons of the wine harvest. But everyone in Chantelle was thinking *vendange* just then. Might those wheels actually have been M. Thaunié's carriage?

If I had been M. Waldeck-Rousseau I would have explored M. Thaunié's alibi more deeply. Does it sound a little like *la Creuse* itself, hollow?

The Autograph[1]

ONCE THERE WAS AN AUTHOR, A FOREIGNER, WHO WENT ON the road on a lecture trip. Everywhere he was asked for autographs. And although this was a fatigue, and even an embarrassment (for either to perform or to evade made him feel equally silly) he was of compliant disposition and tried to do what seemed expected. But he used to think anxiously of neuritis, for his hand was lame.

In one western city the autograph habit seemed to have reached its climax. Evidently someone—the ruthless lecture agent, or the publisher, or the committee of local dames—had pledged him to sign every book in town. Not only books that the audience might bring in, but even stock on demurrage in the shops. So after his talk, and a luncheon at the hotel, he was taken round to all the bookstores (so that no one might be offended) and dutifully wrote his name.

[1]Copyright, 1938, by Saturday Review Associates, Inc.

248

It happened to be rather a long name, but about the time he was wondering whether anyone knew that printing had been invented he was rescued by a genial parson who took him home to tea. Here the visitor learned (after two cups) that many of the congregation had sent their volumes to the rectory to be authenticated and most of the high school students had brought around their little albums. Presently he was called for to be taken to a cocktail party. After a day in which stress divided by strain had come close to an improper fraction (he had risen at dawn in another city to make his forenoon date) the relaxation of prime bourbon was indeed welcome. Before long he was autographing even before anyone asked it, and writing European folk-songs on the wallpaper.

But he was on an imperative schedule, arranged by the ruthless agent, and there was a train he must catch. Now there was just time for him to scour to the hotel where a room had been kindly reserved for him to bathe and change. His frolicsome hosts took him thither, handed him his key and goodbyes were said. Without even halting at the hotel desk he hastened upstairs to repair his privacies. And then, close upon train time, he realized that in the push of travel he had run through his pocket money and would need some for the railroad ticket. He must cash a traveller's cheque.

With his bag, and departure peremptory, he hurried to the cashier. He started to countersign the cheque. After so much exercise his hand had gone numb and he wrote with pain. How different it looked from the easy script of his carefree signature in New York a few weeks before. The cashier looked doubtfully at the paper.

"I'm very sorry," he said, "but it don't look quite kosher. I don't believe we can honor this."

"Lord help us," cried the visitor, or words to that effect, "if the signature's bad it's because I've been writing my name all afternoon."

"Are you registered here?" asked the cashier.

"I don't think I am," said the distracted guest. "Someone engaged a room for me to change in, but it must be in someone else's name; I didn't sign for it."

The cashier consulted an assistant manager. To him also the wretched Foreigner strove to explain. "Why," he said, "I wrote about a hundred autographs in the ballroom of this very hotel this morning and nobody questioned them."

The cashier and the assistant manager had both come on duty in the afternoon and what had happened that morning was no concern of theirs.

"We got into trouble with the express company not long ago," said the manager, "for accepting some phony signatures."

"Try again," suggested the room clerk, who had caught a strong effusion of bourbon from the guest. "Maybe you just had indigestion the first time."

After a terrified look at the clock our hero made another attempt; but nervousness and fatigue had now completely unstrung his members. The signature was worse than before and looked a palpable and clumsy forgery. The manager had half a mind to call the house detective, yet something pitiable in the stranger's demeanor appealed to his humanity.

"Isn't there anyone in town who can identify you?" he asked.

The irony of this, in the same hotel where he had been hailed that morning as wiser than Maeterlinck and funnier than Harry Lauder, did not just then appeal to the visitor. There was now about two minutes leeway. He gazed round the lobby and of course saw no one he knew. Indeed his various hosts and listeners were by now at their comfortable dinner tables, probably talking over his eccentricities and wondering why they had taken the trouble to drag along a book for an autograph.

"Call up Dr. Mansard," he cried feverishly, mentioning the cultured parson of the afternoon tea. "For God's sake hurry, I've got to catch the seven-fifteen." Fearfully he remembered the deep and leisurely solemnity of Dr. Mansard's conversation.

But at that moment a beautiful creature in evening wraps came past the desk. Miracle: he recognized her, and she him. Under her arm she still carried the book he had signed for her in the heyday of his meridian.

"Why, Mr. Sansevieria!" she exclaimed. "Poor soul, what's wrong?"

Quick now; we must move fast. 20 seconds for him to explain; 20 seconds for her to show the cashier the untainted signature he had done earlier; 20 seconds for the manager to accept her assurance. 20 seconds more to count out the money, and 20 seconds to rush him to her car. She drove swiftly to the depot.

"I hope I didn't sound ill-humored," he said. "I really was desperate. I've been saying to myself, if I met a woman who didn't want an autograph I believe I'd fall in love with her. Caramba, I'd give her something better than an autograph."

They pulled up at the station just as the Katy whistled for the curve.

"I'd like you to know," she said, "I didn't ask it for myself. I only wanted it for my kid sister-in-law. That's where I'm taking it now."

"Sister-in-law? What a pity. Your husband's sister."

"No, my sister's husband's sister.— There's your train."

A Letter to T. W. L.

Dear Tom:

I always think of you at Xmas time; partly because I have now got you firmly associated in my mind with that noble little preface by Bishop Stubbs, in the first volume of his *Constitutional History*—which he wrote at Oxford on Xmas Day 1873. "The History of Institutions cannot be mastered,—can scarcely be approached,—without an effort." That, I submit, is a thrilling first sentence, and challenges all one has of attention. As I have so often told you, that big-little preface is my annual Xmas priority.

But I thought particularly of you a few weeks ago (a bright breezy day in early November) when my wife and I went down to spend a day at Canterbury. I wanted to see for myself what had happened to the Cathedral, and I felt you (and Chaucer too, with whom I carry on a sort of secret grapevine

communication) deserve a word of direct report. We spent
the greater part of our time with John Conrad and his family
—he is the younger son of Joseph—he is an architect in Canterbury, lives in a delightful little house he built for himself some
miles south, on the Dover Road. But in the late gold of autumn afternoon, rapidly fading to silvery color like the cathedral itself, we walked round and through the great lonely and
stonely aisles and chapels. How extraordinarily tall the nave
seems, lifting higher and higher above one's gaze in the dusk.

It seems plain that the Luftwaffe must have made serious
attempt to hit the cathedral, for the damage all round it is
bad; it is as miraculous as the survival of St. Paul's. A good
deal of work was going on outside, patching up pinnacles, etc.
Generally speaking, the impression I got was like that of a
magnificent First Edition that has been (as booksellers say)
a bit foxed and shaken; there are certainly stains and scars
on the binding; but the Book Itself unbroken. I was in a mood
for feeling rather than noticing, but I think ourselves and
John Conrad were, at that hour, the only or almost the only
pilgrims. Beyond the great flight of steps, somewhere in the
Choir, was the best kind of worshipper: a solitary workman
on a scaffold quietly painting or regilding a great golden
screen, a thing as full of scales or foliations as a pineapple.
Under an electric bulb he went on steadily with his brush.
(That reminds me that when I went to Southwark Cathedral
with a friend, the only other person we saw was a young
woman down on her knees on the stone flags washing some
of the marble monuments and tablets. She said she does it
regularly, it is her way of helping; but she can't get enough
soap to get the marbles as clean as she wd like. She was at
work just outside the Harvard Chapel when we saw her.)

The only other time I was at Canterbury was some 20 yrs ago, when we drove down in a car (with the H. M. Tomlinsons) to see my other shrine there, J. Conrad's grave—in the R. Catholic cemetery. But to go by train, as we did this time, gives the better approach. The railway makes a long bend on a raised embankment and you get superb first views of the cathedral, rising like a great shout in stone, a sort of oecumenical varsity cheer, from the Kentish fields. It is odd to remember (I think I'm right) that silvery stone was all barged over from Normandy? It must be the biggest chunk of France that England ever took away (for keeps).—I was asking John Conrad whether his father ever showed much interest in the Cathedral, in the many years he lived in that region. Because one was often curious about JC's religious feelings, if any (a matter to which he hardly ever alluded in his writings, public or private). John said he believed his father went into the Cathedral "once or twice, when nobody was about." I thought it odd that when we went to sign the huge visitors' album, the last signature but one before ours was that of a Polish lady from Warsaw. John was much impressed by this (he has a strong feeling for his Polish ancestry, and has built his home in the style of one of the typical small manor-houses of the Ukraine) and signed his own name in full: John Conrad Korzeniowski.

As I saw the workmen on the great scaffolds along the southern flank I thought, of course, of you, and wished you could have seen the great Bell Harry Tower in that pinkening sunset light. It was a pellucid day for seeing great things; we got back to Town pretty late (if you remember the Southern Ry) and had dinner at the last of the unchangeable Victorian hotels, the old Grosvenor—where I am sure the ghosts of Sherlock Holmes and Dr. Watson still attack a ghostly steak-and-kidney pie.

Now the pressure of Xmas begins to encroach; I don't know when this can get mailed (we live a long way from P.O. & ways are slidder as Chaucer wd say) but anyhow there's room to write out for you my this year's carol:—

> Saints and sandals
> Go together,
> They kindle candles
> In Xmas weather.
> Their toes enjoy
> Wide open spaces—
> Saints are too lazy
> To do up laces.

A good Christmas to you all. What a fortunate man you are, to have had—and used—so many opportunities for living and forwarding life.